DON'T
GROW
WEARY

DON'T GROW WEARY

DR. LARRY LINKOUS

CREATION
HOUSE

Don't Grow Weary by Dr. Larry Linkous
Published by Creation House
A Charisma Media Company
600 Rinehart Road
Lake Mary, Florida 32746
www.charismamedia.com

Design Director: Bill Johnson
Cover design by Nathan Morgan

Visit the author's website: www.findnewlife.com

Library of Congress Control Number: 2011942169
International Standard Book Number: 978-1-61638-818-8
E-book International Standard Book Number: 978-1-61638-819-5

While the author has made every effort to provide accurate telephone numbers and Internet addresses at the time of publication, neither the publisher nor the author assumes any responsibility for errors or for changes that occur after publication.

First edition

12 13 14 15 16 — 987654321
Printed in Canada

ACKNOWLEDGMENTS

ALL GLORY AND thanksgiving to Christ my Savior Who has redeemed me and filled my deepest longings.

To my wife Sandra, a special word of deep appreciation and love, not only in relationship to this book, but in all my life and ministry. You are my beautiful and treasured covenant friend.

To my best male friend, my son Jason, my business partner and ministry partner as we "do all things for the sake of the Gospel." To his beautiful wife Mindy, and our two grandsons, Isaak and Elijah, such joys of our hearts.

To my mom who continues on with faith after the loss of my father and her husband of sixty-nine years.

To Rita, my most trusted secretary and assistant. A woman of integrity and faith. You keep me reminded. To Debbie, Sue, Jackie, Cheryl, Sandi, and everyone in the office who has encouraged me along.

To Jack and Meghan. Your work moved me forward out of a manuscript into a book. You are God's gift to Sandra and me.

To my New Life Council, my pastors, secretaries, and all my staff. Thank you for your confidence and support.

To the greatest family of believers in the world who make up New Life Christian Fellowship. I am so honored to be your pastor.

To My Dad, Bishop Malcolm T. Linkous. Gone home to his eternal home with Christ after sixty-seven years of faithful ministry. I miss you more than I imagined. Thank you for all you gave.

To everyone who has brought me correction, love and prayerful support. You have touched and guided my life. I am grateful. To each one who takes the time to read and understand. May God bless you abundantly.

CONTENTS

Introduction 1

Part One: Rest for the Weary

1   A Way Out...5

2   Move That Mountain!..9

3   Tired or Weary? 11

4   Seed Time and Harvest...15

5   Love Feeds 17

6   The Servant Principle...21

7   Live a Life Worth Leaving 25

8   The Lie Whisperer...35

9   Who's in Your Huddle?...41

10 The Power of Words 45

Part Two: The Master's Keys

11 The Master's Keys Revealed....................................53

12 Key #1: The Key of Authority 55

13 Key #2: Pursue Your Assignment 59

14 Key #3: Receive Mercy..69

15 Key #4: Get Understanding 73

16 Key #5: Wait...79

17 Key #6: Repent...81

18 Key #7: Consider Jesus 85

    Conclusion 89

    Notes 95

    About the Author 97

    Contact the Author 99

INTRODUCTION

R EADING RELEASES US from the prison of our own thinking. There are times in our lives when we can become captivated by our own thoughts, clamoring like prisoners in a dungeon for a way out of our mental clutter—clutter that confuses, frustrates, and prevents us from making good decisions. We need help from the outside. We need someone with a key that unlocks the door, revealing the clear way out. Somebody call 9-1-1!

Well, in this book I offer you some keys. They are really not my own; these are the Master's keys I have discovered in the greatest of all books—God's Word. I will help you identify them so you can unlock any shackle that has imprisoned you and shake the weariness that has subtly invaded your mind and has begun suffocating your joy and passion for living.

You used to enjoy life more. You worried less, you laughed easier, and you were kinder. Life and all it brings has worn on you. You have become weary.

I am here to help you overcome that. This is a book about how to not grow weary. Weary is not good. To become weary is to lose heart. But we're not going in that direction. We are going to get your heart and your joy back, because out of your heart flow all the issues of life.

I wrote this book because I believe it will help you win. It will empower you to live a life tracing the fingerprints of God's design for you. I believe it will help you overcome the blunt force trauma of the attack on your life that has come to make you weary and to pressure you to quit. You are not going to quit. The Lord has sent this book across your path on purpose to help you walk in a new dimension of life and freedom. You can get your joy back. You can once again laugh easier. You can regain your kinder and gentler self.

In this process we are going to prayerfully turn to the Lord and find some answers to overcome the heaviness that has draped around you. You will find a place at the altar of our faithful God to lay your burdens down and get on with a great life of fulfillment and joy, the life you were designed to live. I know you will be better off for the time you invest here. You will discover the Master's keys to freedom from your weary, cluttered mind.

PART ONE

REST FOR the WEARY

Chapter 1

A WAY OUT

YOU HAVE FINGERPRINTS on you. You cannot wash them off. They are the fingerprints of God, and they were etched there as He formed you in your mother's womb. In His fingerprint are the design and plan He has for your life. It is a great plan. God says, "'For I know the plans that I have for you,' declares the LORD, 'plans for welfare and not for calamity to give you a future and a hope'" (Jer. 29:11). That's great news!

But there is also bad news: most people never live that plan. God's design and plan for you face an enemy who throws all his diabolical weapons against you to keep you from ever rising to and realizing God's great design for your life. However, he doesn't have the last word. Whether you live your life here on earth fulfilling and experiencing God's plan for your life isn't in your enemy's power, although he will try to convince you it is.

But it isn't in God's power either. It is in your power. You are the one who daily decides whether you are going to walk in the victories God has designed in you and for you or if you are going to walk in defeat and live your life failing and unfulfilled. God has given you the power to win and the weapons to win, but you must choose to walk with Him and use all He has given you to war against the archenemy of your life, your future, and your legacy. Your enemy isn't a figment of your imagination; he has come to "kill, steal, and destroy you." (See John 10:10.)

> Ron Preacher was coming home...from a party celebrating his fifty-third birthday when he received a call from his former wife.
> Their son, Matthew, a decorated army veteran who

recently had returned from his third tour of duty in Iraq, had killed himself earlier that day.

For Preacher, the call in January 2009 started a year-long spiral.

His weight rose to 378 pounds, and he was hospitalized with two heart attacks. He was diagnosed with takotsubo cardiomyopathy—in layman's terms, "broken-heart syndrome"—a stress-induced condition affecting the workings of the heart and often attributed to the loss of a loved one.

Preacher was ready to die like his son.

"I realized that I didn't care anymore about life. I had given up. I felt like I was standing on a cliff," Preacher said, recalling his dark days after Matthew shot himself in his South Carolina apartment. "To lose your son—it knocked the wind out of me. It was kind of a perfect storm."

Instead of using a pistol, he was using food, he said. It was only after seeing his current wife, Karen's, emotional reaction to his doctor's frank prognosis that Preacher decided to give life one more shot.

"I looked over, and my wife started crying," Preacher said. "I finally woke up."

Preacher's story is one of transformation from despair and near-death to a healthier lifestyle. Today, he's 139 pounds lighter, teaching martial arts to children and teens, and trying to help others who may be depressed understand that all is not lost. He recently received national recognition for his efforts.

Preacher's recovery came with the help of Wendy Russo, wellness coordinator and personal trainer at the Titusville YMCA. She gave him a strict regimen of workouts and meal plans.

"She taught me that bacon wasn't a vegetable," Preacher said.

Preacher now eats six small meals a day consisting

of proteins, vegetables, and complex carbohydrates—no sugar. And his workouts include five or six days a week of cardiovascular exercises and three days a week of weight training. He lost more than one hundred pounds within six months.

Before her husband's transformation, Karen Preacher, 37, said, "It was like an abyss. It was depressing. It was dark. We argued a lot. We were going down a really dark street there. You're already in a tailspin, and then you burst into flames. He was dying. I wanted my husband back."

Russo also encouraged Preacher to return to church, where he received spiritual support from Senior Pastor Larry Linkous of New Life Christian Fellowship in Titusville, one of the area's largest churches, with about 1,800 families.

"He's a man on his way to total healing," said Linkous, who met Preacher at the Y. "He has just started, but he has made a life commitment out of it. It's amazing what happened to him. He inspires me, and I am proud to be his pastor."

Preacher told his story on Linkous' morning call-in radio show, and the response was overwhelming.

"You can tell if you've reached people by the lights on the phone lines," Linkous said.

Those lights continually blinked that morning, with people on hold waiting to talk with Preacher. Some, encouraged by Preacher's words and actions, resolved to turn their lives around as well.

Preacher tells the story of his downfall and recovery in hopes it will help others.

Preacher recently was named one of ten "special honors achievement" winners in a national Transformation Challenge program coordinated by fitness expert Bill Phillips, who is known for his *Body for Life* best seller and the recently released *Transformation*.

"I've learned that I could help other people who are at the end of their rope," Preacher said.

"We want to give hope to the people who think they have reached the end," Karen Preacher said.

And he now wants to help people in need. He strikes up conversations with strangers he sees out shopping and tells them about his experiences.

"I'm more giving now, and I actually like my life right now," Preacher said. "God just lifted me up. I realize there's always hope. There's always a way out."[1]

Most likely none of us face a weary condition as dramatic as Ron's. But if you are allowing any event in your life to drain your vigor and joy of living, then you are in need of this book.

Ron says, "There's always a way out. There's always hope." As we work our way through God's promises in this book, you will find hope, and that hope will be your doorway out.

By the way, that national Transformation Challenge program by fitness expert Bill Phillips was held in Denver, Colorado, in November of 2010. Out of more than three thousand participants, Ron Preacher won the award. He is now on Bill Phillips's staff and represents him and the Transformation Program globally. "There's always a way out."

...let us lay aside every weight, and the sin which so easily ensnares us, and let us run with endurance the race that is set before us.

—Hebrews 12:1, nkjv

Chapter 2

MOVE THAT MOUNTAIN!

I RECALL AS A child traveling with my parents out of Chattanooga, Tennessee, on a highway that immediately faced the challenge of the steep inclines of the famous Lookout Mountain. My dad was a pastor, and he also traveled extensively to preach. Traveling with my mom, my dad, and my older brother, I always found these road trips to be a source of excitement.

The roads were just two lanes winding up the steep mountainside, and we would inevitably get caught in a line of slow-moving semitrailer trucks. Under the weight of their heavy loads these trucks were barely able to creep up the great mountain. Some would pull over with their radiators boiling over, not able to handle the extreme terrain. These trucks had great engines and could have negotiated the mountain quite well except for the heavy weight they were attempting to pull up the mountain.

I realize now that the answer to these truckers' problems was not unlike the answer to the problems we face today on our life journeys—*either move the mountain or lighten the load.*

Jesus said that if we have the right ingredients in our faith, we can move mountains, and just like He said, there have been times when we have had strong faith, prayed, and saw mountains move. It was miraculous! What a celebration. We cherish these mountain-moving experiences.

However, much of the time, and maybe most of the time, we have to deal with the mountains in our lives in more mundane earthly ways. The earthly way requires lightening the load. In each of our lives we must deal with the issues that bring hardship and challenges to our journey. These hardships can amass burden on our lives and hinder our progress toward our designed and desired goals. Not only can it hinder our progress to our goals, but the heavy weight can also cause us to lose sight of the goal and throw us into a wilderness of wandering and frustration. You weren't designed for the extra weight. We add weights to our lives so gradually that we don't realize how much has accumulated in our minds and emotions. We begin to accept the struggle as normal. But it isn't normal, and we must recognize the load we are carrying is destructive and find a way and a place to lay it aside. Jesus entreats us to "[cast] all our anxiety [burdens] on Him, because He cares for you" (1 Pet. 5:7). If we do, we seldom leave them there because in reality we don't trust Him with them as much as we trust ourselves. But this part of our lives is no game. It is critical. If we don't lighten the load, whatever we are carrying and attempting to bear up under will grind our hopes and dreams into the ground. We must find a way to unload wearisome baggage. It's weighing us down and boiling over, and soon we will be pulled over beside the road of life with everyone passing us by.

This fight is serious. The weight brings turmoil and opens you to spiritual, mental, and emotional attack, but "no temptation has overtaken you but such as is common to man; and God is faithful, who will not allow you to be tempted beyond what you are able, but with the temptation will provide the way of escape also, so that you will be able to endure it" (1 Cor. 10:13).

Chapter 3

TIRED OR WEARY?

U NTIL NOW, YOU may have considered *tired* and *weary* to be synonymous. They are not. When you are tired, you are dealing with the physical realm. Being tired means you need physical rest or a break, some sleep, and quite possibly a vacation. If you are tired, you may need to change some life habits. You may need to exercise or exercise differently. Perhaps you have a physical problem that needs medical attention. The point is, tired is physical. You cannot pray tired away. You do not rebuke tired. You cannot lay hands on someone and cast out tired.

What we are discussing in this book is not about tired; it is about weary. Weary is *spiritual*. Although tired and weary may at times feel closely related, they are worlds apart. Tired is physical; weary is spiritual. Weary does not respond to the same treatment as tired. You can go away for a month to rest and relax, but you may still be weary. The Greek word translated "weary" is *ekkakeô*. It is used in the sense of being in the midst of misfortune, to be unfortunate, desperate; it is often translated "to lose heart." As the New King James Version reads, "And let us not grow weary while doing good, for in due season we will reap if we do not lose heart" (Gal. 6:9). This verse is talking about spiritual weariness.

If you are weary, you have in the past or are now experiencing some upheaval or crisis in your life that has damaged you, and you have not yet recovered from the damage. Each of us has had these places in our lives—places of difficulty, despair, discouragement, disillusionment, and disappointment. In some of these places we have given up, thrown up our hands, and quit when we should have pressed in to success. If we would have persevered, we could have realized the harvest from the seed we had invested in that relationship, job, venture, or idea. However, we became weary in the battle and fell into the trap, thus throwing up our hands, giving up, and walking away. We lose heart and quit. But according to Galatians 6:9, we do not have to quit or give in. We can get the strength we need from God to lay aside the extra weight and carry on into victory.

If you are battling for your marriage, let me encourage you to hang in there. Even if you have to remove yourself from the household to allow a time of counsel, reflection, and healing, give your marriage everything you can. Consider the seed you have sown there—the years, your youth, your children, your love, your passion—your very life. I was impacted by the words of a counselor friend of mine teaching a class on forgiveness. Speaking of a spouse who had been the victim of infidelity, he said "You have the right to divorce, but you also have the right to forgive." Forgiveness is big. Be sure you sow a lot of forgiveness into your marriage. There may be times you cannot stay in a relationship, but be sure you have exhausted every option.

During the 2008 presidential debates mediator Pastor Rick Warren of Saddleback Church asked both presidential candidates what they considered the most regretful failures of their past life. John McCain answered immediately and without hesitation that his greatest failure was his lack of a greater commitment to preserving his first marriage. He seems to have a good marriage today, but I thought he was quite candid when he shared his realization that, looking back over the years, he could have tried harder. He left a lot of seed in the ground. There is no worthwhile relationship that can exist without large, continuous doses of forgiveness, grace, and mercy—especially a marriage relationship. Be sure you are bringing those ingredients to the table in all of your relationships. Forgiveness is good seed, and it produces a marvelous harvest of forgiveness back into your life. You reap what you sow.

Through this book I hope to give you the tools and resources you need to move past your state of weariness, because when you continue in your own strength, you will fall under the weight. Then, by default, you will find yourself quitting before you've reaped. You do not want to leave any seed in the ground "unharvested." A truly satisfied life comes from knowing you have maximized all that God has for you, and He has so much for you to enjoy. He has an abundant life for you—already paid for. It is in His plan to help you through whatever it is so that you can know going through it that you are doing all you can to claim every promise and every blessing He has for you, including a successful marriage, a satisfying career, fulfilled relationships with family and friends, financial peace, and so much more.

Chapter 4

SEED TIME AND HARVEST

CONSIDER HOW MUCH of your life you have spent sowing. A lot of it, to be certain, more than you may realize. Think about it: you have good seed in the ground. You have loved, you have given, you have stood strong, you have prayed, and you have been faithful. That is all good seed. So guess what? You have a harvest on the way! Therefore you can't quit. The moment you give up is the moment you walk away from your harvest. If you could look at the span of your life on a map, you would see that down the road in your future your harvest is springing up!

Your enemy wants your harvest. He doesn't want it because it will profit him; he just does not want you to have it. Jesus says, "The devil comes only to steal and kill and destroy; I came that they might have life, and have it abundantly" (John 10:10). The devil wants you to quit so he can destroy your harvest. Your seed will harvest, but you must be sure you are in the right place to reap it.

John Eldredge says, "Before He promised us life, Jesus warned that a thief would try to steal, kill, and destroy it. How come we don't think that the thief then actually kills, steals, and destroys? You won't understand your life; you won't see clearly what has happened to you or how to live forward from here unless you see it as a battle—a war against your heart. And you are going to need your whole heart for what's coming next. I don't mean what's coming next in the story I'm telling. I mean what's coming next in the life you're living....The story of your life is the story of a long and brutal assault on your heart by the one who knows what you could be and fears it."[1]

Again, Galatians 6:9 says, "And let us not be weary in well doing: for in due season we shall reap, if we faint not" (KJV). This verse is the centerpiece of this book. When you enter this verse, you enter

15

into an agricultural arena. The words *season* and *reap* are clues to where the writer is taking us in this thought process. We find ourselves knee deep in soybeans or lost in a cornfield. We are sowing and reaping.

The Bible teaches us that "while the earth remains, seedtime and harvest, and cold and heat, and summer and winter, and day and night, shall not cease" (Gen. 8:22). The scripture relates harvest with the earth. I believe for the most part that rewards are related to what we receive in heaven, and harvest is related to what we reap from our sowing while here on earth.

The great gift of Jesus Christ as our Savior and the eternal life He brings are gifts God gives freely. You didn't sow anything to receive this great gift of salvation. It is God's free gift to everyone who believes.

> Even when we were dead in sins, hath quickened us together with Christ, (by grace ye are saved;)...For by grace are ye saved through faith; and that not of yourselves: it is the gift of God: Not of works, lest any man should boast.
> —Ephesians 2:5, 8–9, kjv

If you have given your life to Christ and have received Him as your personal Savior, then the jury is in on your eternal destiny. You will spend your eternity with Christ in His glorious kingdom. However, the jury is still out on how much heaven you will experience while you're still here on earth. That will be determined in a large sense by *how much* and *what* you sow. Heaven on earth depends very much on the seed you're plowing into the earth. We do sow and reap, and we reap what we sow.

So when Paul speaks of being weary, he is not concerned with us losing our eternal life with Christ. He's concerned about our earthly life, that we do not lose our harvest. "Don't grow weary in doing well, for we shall reap if we do not faint."

Chapter 5

LOVE FEEDS

Recently I pulled into a gas station for a fill-up. When I swiped my card at the pump, I inadvertently initiated a conversation: "Please enter your area code," the pump read. That was fine; I appreciated the protection of my credit. However, next came, "Do you want a receipt?" "Do you want debit or credit?" "Do you want a car wash?" By the time I got to answering "Do you want a liter of Pepsi?" I was running quite low on patience. I had come for gasoline; I did not need to become so acquainted with the gas pump.

This incident served to remind me that everything in life comes with demands. Every situation, every relationship, and each circumstance will demand something of you and expect a response. You will respond. You will either respond out of your fleshly emotions, or you will respond out of your redeemed overflow.

Jesus had a most interesting encounter with Peter. This encounter took place after Jesus's resurrection and before His ascension. We discover Christ on the sandy shores of Galilee cooking breakfast for the disciples as they were fishing. As they brought their boats to shore and drew nearer to Him, they recognized it was Jesus. He had come specifically for a pointed conversation with Peter. Peter had recently denied Jesus three times, and his Lord had come to restore him and to give Peter his life's assignment.

> When they had finished eating, Jesus said to Simon Peter, "Simon son of John, do you truly love me more than these?" "Yes, Lord," he said, "you know that I love you." Jesus said, "Feed my lambs." Again Jesus said "Simon son of John, do you truly love me?" He answered, "Yes, Lord, you know that I love you." Jesus said, "Take care of my

17

sheep." The third time he said to him "Simon son of John, do you love me?" Peter was hurt because Jesus asked him the third time "Do you love me?" He said, "Lord, you know all things; you know that I love you." Jesus said, "Feed my sheep."

—JOHN 21:15–17, NIV

The question Jesus asked Peter pricked his heart. I can see Jesus gesture with His nail-scarred hand, a motion that included everything important to Peter. As He motioned, Jesus said, "Peter, do you love Me more that these?" Understand what "these" represented. Here was Peter's business: his boats and nets, his employees, his friends and partners, his financial security, safety for his family's future, his profits—everything he had ever worked for. "Do you love Me more than these?" "Yes, Lord, you know I love You" was Peter's answer. Jesus responded, "If you love Me, feed My sheep." Now that the relationship had been made right, Jesus gave Peter his lifelong assignment: "Feed My sheep."

Love feeds. Negative emotions drain. When you respond to the demands of friends, family, and even strangers on the street, you must remember Christ's command to feed. If you respond with a lack of self-control, impatience, or anger, you are not feeding them or yourself. Love feeds. Joy feeds. Patience feeds. Understand that every circumstance in your life today will demand something of you. You will respond to each of these draining demands by either offering them something of love and value or by responding in your flesh and out of your emotional emptiness. If you cast your cares on Jesus as we discussed in a previous chapter, letting Him carry your burdens and give you rest, you will respond in love, and your love will feed.

Stephen Covey, in his book *Seven Habits for Highly Effective Families*, teaches that between the stimulus and the response is a space—a space where you have the opportunity to decide how you will respond. You control your response. No one *makes* you mad. We sometimes say, "They made me so mad!" Not true.

If in your space between the stimulus and your response you decided to respond in anger, then you must consider how the response you make is going to affect your future. I have seen people win an argument but lose their future.

As you grow the space between the stimulus and response, you will better preserve the quality of your relationships and the quality of your life. If you can find the patience and control to wait before you react, your response is more likely to be a winning one—one that feeds and one that brings glory to God, honor to others, and dignity to you. Otherwise, you are reacting out of your carnal emotions and bringing hurt and embarrassment. A soulish response limits the fruitfulness of relationships that should have otherwise enriched your life.

Hollywood and Madison Avenue marketing has filled our minds with erroneous beliefs. People look for someone to marry who will fill their lives and fulfill their every grand desire. We are taught to marry someone because of what he or she can give or what he or she brings to us. It only takes a glance at the failure rate in marriages to see what a weak foundation this kind of thinking produces. Love feeds. If our marriages are to succeed, we must come to grips with the fact that we do not have the right to demand; neither do our spouses have the ability to fulfill all our demands and needs.

God created each of us with a vacuum inside of us, a hole in our soul that can only be filled by a redeemed relationship with Him. Only Christ can satisfy our deepest longings and fill that vacuum in our souls.

As we grow into maturity, we learn that our marriages or any meaningful relationship cannot survive our demands. Love feeds. Any relationship that is lasting and meaningful is one we feed with love. However, we must first be filled with the love and life of God. Only then can we bring love and life to our marriage. We bring something. We feed our relationships. We have something to offer. We no longer demand of another what only God can do for us. Out of a true and proper relationship with Christ, we will fulfill His assignment and enjoy full and meaningful lives.

We should ask ourselves these questions: How did I affect the encounter I just had? Is that person I just encountered better off or worse off because I was there? Did I deposit something that made his/her life better, or did I withdraw something? When I leave people, have I added something of value to their lives, or have I taken something of value away? Am I the kind of person someone enjoys sitting by? Would someone desire to join me at the table?

Recently I was speaking to a group of about two hundred men I mentor at the church. I call them Mighty Men after David's mighty men. I challenged each of them to go and ask his family, "Am I a safe place?" We all want to be a part of a safe place. We want our friendships, our employee relationships, our churches, and our homes to be safe places where our children and our families can be comfortable and grow into healthy, mature individuals.

The only way I can create a safe place is to first of all be a safe place. I must be sure I'm a safe place for my wife. She must feel safe with me and around me. She has to know I'm true to her and her alone. She must be sure that I will never purposefully embarrass her, scorn her, humiliate her, and uncover her. I must be a place she can come to and talk and rest and know she's safe in my love and acceptance. I must be that same kind of friend, pastor, father, and brother. The only way there will be a safe place is that it centers up, around, and in me. The safe place starts here.

Even though you are going through a time of weariness and being overwhelmed, know that getting what you need to overcome this time starts with you. It starts with you going to Jesus, who can give you the rest and restoration that you need. He will fill you up so that you are able to feed those around you and be a safe place for your most significant relationships. You need the special people in your life, so responding to them out of your emptiness is not an option. In order to be obedient to Christ and feed His sheep, you must operate out of the endless well of His love and strength. One way to do that is by serving them, which is what we'll discuss in the next chapter.

Chapter 6

THE SERVANT PRINCIPLE

A SPECIAL PRINCIPLE I attempt to live by is found in the lines of a verse written by Paul in his letter to the Corinthians: "Though I am free and belong to no man, I make myself a slave to everyone, to win as many as possible" (1 Cor. 9:19, NIV). Did you catch the principle? It is rather hidden. Here it is: *If you want it, serve it.*

Paul says, "I don't have to do all this. I'm a Christian saved by grace. I can stay in Antioch and live my life out fully and die here and go to heaven. I am free from all. However, my life is bigger than that. I have made myself a servant to all so I can win those I serve" (author's paraphrase).

I have found in my life (for the most part) that what I serve, I win. If I want my marriage to be rewarding and fulfilling, I must serve it. If I want a covenant relationship with my son, I must serve him. If I want a great church in my community, I must serve it. If I want a great community in my church, I must serve it.

When we started our church in 1983, it wasn't long until I realized we had very few people with babies in the church. We didn't have many people anyway, but hardly any babies. I made a plan to decorate and staff a small nursery for infants and toddlers. Some people looked at me oddly and asked, "Pastor, why are you creating a nursery when we don't have any babies?" I answered, "The reason we don't have babies is because we don't have a nursery." When we started the nursery, families with babies started showing up! And they stayed.

If you want it, serve it. A few years ago a group of us attended a motivational conference in Orlando at the convention center. One of the speakers was Dick Vitale. He said that if he were young again, he would find the corporation that he wanted to work in and invest

21

his life and time into that corporation. He would just show up regularly to volunteer and work excellently in the job assignment. He said he would become so indispensable to the corporation that the powers in charge would have to notice him and realize they couldn't do without him and would begin to pay him to stay. He said from there he would work his way upward.

I know this works. I have pastors on my staff who showed up as volunteers. One of my pastors retired from the navy and came into the church office and asked what he could do. We gave him the membership list and directed him to call every family on the list and encourage them in the Lord, pray for them, and ask how we could better serve them. He did the job. Day after day, this man was on the job doing excellent ministry. I realized how invaluable an asset he was to the ministry and asked what it would take to keep him on the team. I said we didn't have the budget for another staff pastor, but we would do whatever we could within our ability. He came back and told me that if we could pay his grocery bill weekly he could stay. We found that much money in the budget and brought him on staff. Twelve years later this man is still one of our valued pastors.

My wife, Sandra, is my best friend. Our son, Jason, is my best man friend. Jason is married to his beautiful wife, Mindy, with two sons of their own, Isaak and Elijah. For fifteen years he served as copastor of our church, and we are partners in our radio ventures, Daystar Inc. Jason is an invaluable part of my life, our ministry, and our friendship.

That didn't happen accidentally. When Jason was a young man, he chose to focus his athletic ability and attention on tennis. Florida is a major state in tennis because of, among many reasons, the climate. Sandra and I supported and even encouraged his decision totally. It wasn't always easy.

Jason had been discovered by the high school tennis team at the age of twelve, and practiced with them from that point on. He also played United States Tennis Association (USTA) tennis, which demanded much travel around the area. We were his transportation.

Anytime he could enter a tournament that had the competition to elevate his game and his standing in the nation, he would enter. Sandra and I were excited to spend our Saturdays supporting him at his matches. If he won, and he won most of the time, he would play the finals on Sunday. Now this could cause a schedule conflict, because I pastored a growing church. Sunday is important to church. Sometimes I would drive Jason to his semifinal and final matches, two or three hours away, early on Sunday morning. I would leave him at the courts early, even when no one had arrived as yet. I had to drive back the two or three hours to preach at 9:00 a.m. at church. As soon as church was over, Sandra and I would rush back to the tennis match to watch him and support him in the finals.

It was an exciting time in our lives. It was difficult, but it was joyous to us. We loved it. There are no words to describe how very much this season of our lives meant to all of us. However, I think there were few parents so ready for their son to turn sixteen so he could drive himself as we were.

Jason's commitment and ability helped him to the victory of a Florida State Championship in singles and doubles match play his senior year in high school and a full tennis scholarship at Flagler College in St. Augustine. Did I say Jason is my best man friend? That is no accident. If you want it, serve it.

I know that's a different kind of story than some you hear about preachers or corporate executives who were so focused on their work that they ultimately lost their family. Those are tragic stories: good men who meant well but lost focus on their priorities. You need to embrace this list of priorities:

1. God

2. You

3. Your spouse

4. Your children

5. Your work

I put *you* right after God because unless you are in right relationship with God and healed of your old world wounds, you will never love and serve out of a healed and whole position. Without a right relationship with the Lord, you will be demanding of others what only God can give.

When our church was small, Sandra and I would go to conferences and pastoral gatherings to learn how to be better leaders and church-growth facilitators. Many times pastors would talk about how many sons in the faith they were mentoring—ten or twelve or twenty. I would tell the Lord that I didn't have ten or twelve or twenty people in the church, much less twenty disciples in ministry. He reminded me that in those early years my family was my mentoring responsibility. The Lord blessed me for being faithful there even though I wasn't aware of all I was doing.

The Lord is faithful. Jesus says be faithful in the little things. Wherever you are today, however small or insignificant it may seem, don't despise it. Be faithful, be responsible, be accountable, and be excellent with what is in your hand, and the Lord will bring your life great harvest. You reap what you sow. If you want it, serve it. Don't grow weary in doing well, for in due season you will reap if you do not faint. Don't quit!

Chapter 7

LIVE A LIFE WORTH LEAVING

I T MAY NOT seem the world has found you or beat a path to your door, but don't grow weary in what you are doing today. Be faithful. Do what you do excellently even though it may seem no one notices. *SomeOne* notices. You have an audience of One. If you preach, write, paint, sing...if you are in sales, research and development, construction, the military, law enforcement...if you are a first responder, a teacher, a secretary, an engineer, a spouse, a parent...whatever you do, do it excellently and passionately as unto the Lord. He notices and He cares. You will live to realize and enjoy the harvest and blessings of God, but be aware also that all of the results of your work, all the harvest of your seed, may not be revealed until far beyond your earthly life. This is about you but not *just* about you. Your life is about now but not *just* about now.

I am certain that at the time of the apostle Paul's death, although he was lonely and abandoned and it didn't seem the world had found him, he knew he had been found by the One who matters most. Somewhere inside of Paul there must have been some disappointment. Surely his end wasn't the one he would have chosen, but he could have had no idea that his complete and unrelenting service to the vision and the revelation of Christ on the road to Damascus would frame the entire New Testament church for all time. He couldn't have known that the thirteen letters he wrote to deal with the most divisive and destructive problems and heresies in the churches he founded would serve as New Testament Holy Scripture. How could he have known that throughout the New Testament dispensation he would dispense grace and guide church leaders in their crises? Or that his writings would be embraced and revered as Bible doctrine exemplary for every Christian's life and be used as structure for every New Testament church?

25

He knew he had fought the fight, kept the faith, and remained obedient to the high heavenly calling on his life. But there was no way he could have ever dreamed of his far-reaching, cosmic-invading impact on the lives of millions of men and women. Men and women have used his words as fundamental principles, guiding them into great wealth and success, or others in their lonely and broken state would fumble through some crumpled New Testament pages and through teary, hopeless eyes look upon a verse written by Paul in his own crisis. "What shall we say to these things? If God is for us who is against us?" (Rom. 8:31), or "...in all these things we overwhelmingly conquer through Him who loved us" (Rom. 8:37), or words like "Be anxious for nothing" (Phil. 4:6).So, what about you? The whole of your life is grander than this brief moment of weariness and being overwhelmed with what you are facing. You were chosen and redeemed of God and designed for greatness in His eyes and in His plan. There's no way you can see all that right now. The trials, barriers, and turmoil of this world will blind your eyes to reality. Your enemy—the enemy of your soul, your marriage, your success, your children, and your harvest—wants you to quit. But your loving Savior reaches to you and calls to you to take that next step, breathe that next breath, make that next plan, and dream that next dream. Don't quit!

Think of the parents of Dr. Billy Graham, Winston Churchill, Condoleezza Rice, Ronald Reagan, Martin Luther King Jr., Mother Theresa, or Oral Roberts who were raising and forming great men and women who would shape the future of the world.

When Mama Graham was awakened in the night with a crying baby, or Papa Graham was struggling with finances during the Great Depression on the dairy farm to feed his family, did they ever imagine their efforts, trials, and tribulations would produce a preacher who would win millions to Christ by the preaching of the gospel throughout the world? They didn't see the stadiums filled with families and the infields filled with thousands coming to Christ through Billy Graham's invitation. No, they were just faithful to their responsibilities. They didn't quit. Their love, their hope for the future, their commitment to legacy moved them forward.

These were men and women who "did not receive what was promised." They believed in a promise beyond themselves—a promise that was fully realized in their children and grandchildren, a promise that is being fulfilled even today.

Because those before us refused to give up, even though weary, we have hope and we have a future. Not only do we have our own future, but also our determination, our steadfastness, and our faith—faith like the heroes of faith in Hebrews 11—will birth a future for those beyond us, those we will never see, who "apart from us will not be complete."

There were many times, without doubt, that the list of heroes of faith in Hebrews 11—or my list of heroes or your list of heroes—considered giving up. They all grew weary as you have. Many times. But they refused to quit. To quit would have been selfish and self-serving. Heroes live a life beyond themselves. They thought of you and me, and even though giving up may have at the moment seemed easier, they refused easier and lived on to serve us. Life is hard sometimes. Life is every day. But your life is bigger than now. Your steadfastness and your faithful determination serves beyond what you see.

Remember Paul's statement: "For though I am free from all men, I have made myself a slave to all, so that I may win more." Paul realized he didn't have to travel, toil, suffer, encounter hardships, rejection, beatings, shipwreck, despair, hunger, pain, prison, and hatred from inside and outside the church. "I don't have to do this, any of this. I'm free from all. I'm a Christian. Putting up with these Judaizers and their heresy doesn't make me a Christian. Suffering rejection in prison doesn't make me a Christian. I'm free! The blood of Jesus has bought my salvation, and I acknowledge and receive His great redemption for me. I can sit here in Antioch around my friends and talk about Scripture all day long. I can sit here on the sofa and eat bologna sandwiches and drink ice tea until I die from high cholesterol. I'm free from it all" (author's paraphrase).

But something higher, greater, and loftier was burning inside of Paul that wouldn't allow him to sit there, to fellowship there, to stay there until he died. There was a higher voice, a loftier call that moved him out of himself and into the service of all mankind.

No person other than Jesus Christ Himself has affected all mankind around the world and has impacted every Christian more than the apostle Paul. Paul received and interprets the revelation of grace, a revelation given to him personally by Christ Himself. Paul's theology and his ministry delivered and transformed the church from the danger of becoming a narrow sect of old law religion into a dynamic, Spirit-filled, world-changing evangelistic outreach based in and gushing out of Antioch. Because of Paul and God's spotlight on his life the world headquarters of the New Testament church moved from Jerusalem to Antioch. And from that time forward everything that Paul did became the centerpiece of God's attention and subject of the words penned on New Testament parchment by the gifted ability of Luke. Paul capsulated some of his life in these words:

> In far more labors, in far more imprisonments, beaten times without number, often in danger of death. Five times I received from the Jews thirty-nine lashes. Three times I was beaten with rods, once I was stoned, three times I was shipwrecked, a night and a day I have spent in the deep. I have been on frequent journeys, in dangers from rivers, dangers from robbers, dangers from my countrymen, dangers from the Gentiles, dangers in the city, dangers in the wilderness, dangers on the sea, dangers among false brethren; I have been in labor and hardship, through many sleepless nights, in hunger and thirst, often without food, in cold and exposure. Apart from such external things, there is the daily pressure on me of concern for all the churches.
>
> —2 Corinthians 11:23–28

Do you know what he says about it? "I don't have to do this. I'm free. But I make myself a slave to all so I can win!!" If you want it—serve it.

Among so many things that jump off the pages of Paul's letter from prison to his beloved partners in Philippi are two rather hidden truths that capture me. The first is in his letter to the Philippians:

> Now I want you to know, brothers, that what has happened to me has really served to advance the gospel. As a result, it has become clear throughout the whole palace guard and to everyone else that I am in chains for Christ.
>
> —Philippians 1:12–13, niv

When Paul was in prison in Rome the first time he was treated rather well and could write with this kind of joy and anticipation in his attitude here. He was imprisoned but allowed to rent a place close to the prison and received visits and ministered and fellowshiped freely in his rented apartment. All this time however Paul was chained to a praetorian guard. Most likely on a regular basis throughout the day the guards would change duty and another guard would join himself by chains to Paul. In the prison-guard mentality they were chaining Paul to themselves. In Paul's mentality he was chaining them to him! Every shift change gave Paul an opportunity to preach this precious gospel of Jesus Christ and his revelation of grace to another guard to the point that instead of being defeated and pessimistic and self-centered, he says, "What has happened to me has really served to advance the gospel" (v. 12). In other words, "They will know because they've been chained to me" (my translation). Talk about a "captive" audience!

The second interesting insight is revealed in these words: "Greet all the saints in Christ Jesus. The brothers who are with me send greetings. All the saints send you greetings, especially those who belong to Caesar's household" (Phil. 4:21–22, niv). Again we see the infectious passion and testimony of Paul. Paul has won to Christ much of the household of Caesar! His selflessness, his passion, his mission, and his love convict me. He, like each of us who has received Christ, was free from all men but his sofa was not comfortable. He became a slave to all men so he could win some. He won many. He wins me.

Many Bible scholars agree that the apostle Paul was in prison in Rome not once but twice. We have clear biblical historical accounting of two years of Paul's imprisonment in Rome recorded by Luke as he concludes the Book of Acts with these final words:

> And he stayed two full years in his own rented quarters and was welcoming all who came to him, preaching the kingdom of God and teaching concerning the Lord Jesus Christ with all openness, unhindered.
>
> —Acts 28:30–31

From these two verses along with Paul's letters to the Philippians and Ephesians from this term in prison, it truly doesn't seem he is about to face capital punishment. The tone of these epistles is more encouraging than the words of someone who is out of prison! Paul is elated to be in Rome, the capital of the world, the city of his most desired attainment to preach the gospel, and from his words to the Philippians and Ephesians written from Rome, it is evident that although in chains, he is freely preaching the gospel of Jesus Christ and powerfully impacting the city. It is evident by his own admission that he expected to be dismissed and to soon return to these converts he so deeply loved and appreciated.

> Convinced of this, I know that I will remain and continue with you all for your progress and joy in the faith, so that your proud confidence in me may abound in Christ Jesus through my coming to you again.
>
> —Philippians 1:25–26

There is no way to know for sure that Paul was released from prison shortly after the conclusion of the Acts account but many biblical inferences and extra-biblical accounts give us sufficient insight into Paul's final years to believe he was released and had another five years of successful ministry before his second arrest and subsequent execution in Rome either late in A.D. 67 or early in 68. Whether Paul was imprisoned once or twice in Rome, it becomes unquestionably evident that the tone of his letters changes dramatically from his early prison epistles to his final letter to Timothy. This letter wasn't written from a rented apartment where Paul was free to have visitors, it was written from the Mymertine dungeon— "A cold, desolate, and wretched prison reserved for desperate criminals."[1] He writes his final words, and even though final, they are without apology or regret.

> For I am already being poured out as a drink offering, and the time of my departure has come. I have fought the good fight, I have finished the course, I have kept the faith; in the future there is laid up for me the crown of righteousness, which the Lord, the righteous Judge, will award to me on that day; and not only to me, but also to all who have loved His appearing.
>
> —2 TIMOTHY 4:6–8

I can see Paul there placed deep in the depths of this cold dungeon. The cloak he requested has possibly not arrived on time, nor have the parchments. He is cold and shivering, underfed except for some extra food Luke might have been able to pass to him through the barred dungeon doors. He has endured much in his magnificent cause for Christ and the damp and cold of the dungeon serves to amplify the pain and ache of his scarred, possibly crippled body. He has been abandoned by trusted partners. His eyes had been affected early on in his missionary campaigns and when he would get caught in the intensive heat of the Asian summers sickness would impair his sight. (See Galatians 4:15.) But none of this could prevent him from releasing the Holy Spirit-inspired words that burned in him to Timothy.

I see him at the lone rough-hewn table in the corner of the tiny cell saturated with the cold and dampness and stench of the dungeon. See him move as close as he can to the flickering candle so what was left of his sight could guide his shivering hand in those final efforts to pour forth his last instructions and encouragement and directions to Timothy. And as tragic as it was that Timothy quite possibly didn't get back in time to see Paul once again and to fulfill his last desire for some added warmth and comfort, it serves the church so well that these words that could have been lost forever in a personal conversation with Timothy were written and are settled in the Scripture forever for our learning. But don't think these are words of a defeated, disappointed man or a victim, not at all. Paul continues: "But the Lord stood with me and strengthened me, so that through me the proclamation might be fully accomplished, and that all the Gentiles might hear; and I was rescued out of the lion's mouth. The Lord will rescue me from every evil deed, and will bring me safely to His heavenly kingdom; to Him be the glory forever and ever. Amen" (2 Tim. 4:17–18).

> Looking back over more than thirty years of service to the Lord, who called him on the Damascus road, he has no regrets. He would do it all again. He has suffered more than most men; it has cost him much; but he has gained more than he has lost. The long, hard fight is over now. He is not afraid of the outcome. The Lord, his righteous judge, loves him and will take him home. This is the song of triumph of a great warrior who is soon to lose his life but who has won his cause. Paul still has interest in earthly affairs, but his heart is in the hills on high. He looks away to the mountains. His feet are growing restless and the sun is setting in the west. Jesus is beckoning to him and he will go.

> We have no details of the condemnation of Paul by the Roman court. It probably came quickly. If he were accused of complicity in the burning of the city the judgment

would be rendered at once. Since he was a Roman citizen he would not be burned nor cast to the lions; he would be beheaded. At last the sentence of death was pronounced; the great apostle was taken out to the place of execution where he lost his life and gained his crown. He was led out of the city with a crowd of the lowest rabble at his heels. The fatal spot was reached; he knelt beside the block; the headsman's axe gleamed in the sun and fell; and the head of the apostle of the world rolled down in the dust.

So sin did its uttermost and its worst. Yet how poor and empty was its triumph! The blow of the axe only smote off the lock of the prison and let the spirit go forth to its home and to its crown.[2]

When you accept the higher calling of God in Christ Jesus, you will begin to have vision beyond the circumstances of this life. You will be living above what is presently happening to you. The weariness will somehow become an afterthought. Your trials will become a stepping-stone to the promise God has for you and future generations on the other side. You will mount up with the strength of God to overcome and have faith that you will see the victory that is yours.

When you think about those who persevered before you, you will see that you are now persevering for those—your children and their children—who will come after you. If you stay the course and not lose heart just like Paul, Billy Graham, and many others, you will see the fruit of a life well lived.

Chapter 8

THE LIE WHISPERER

THE STRENGTH WE see in and gain from Paul in his most lonely hours is most remarkable. We sense no hint of wavering, no shadow of vulnerability, no shifting of purpose. We watch him come to grips with his feelings toward Alexander the coppersmith and with everyone who had disappointed him and deserted him at his first defense in court. Paul throws off any offense and possible root of bitterness. He evidently stood alone but knew the Source of his strength and the purpose of his tribulations and saw that purpose—"that the Gentiles might hear" (2 Tim. 4:17)—fully accomplished.

Paul is at peace with all his life's issues as he faces his final contest, and it was so important that he was. Any offense, any root of bitterness, and any unforgiveness would have left him vulnerable and could have opened him to defeat rather than bringing him this resounding victory as he faces his final days.

Among the many dangers of growing weary and failing to deal with issues causing your weariness is the heightened level of vulnerability. Whatever has damaged you and caused you to lose heart along your journey only becomes amplified and more critical as the pressures of these conflicts grind you into vulnerability. At this precarious place the enemy of your harvest has plans for you. He sees that your weariness has made you vulnerable, and he intends to destroy your heart. He intends for you to quit. If he can destroy your heart, he can steal your harvest!

The word *vulnerable* means:[1]

+ Susceptible to being wounded

+ Without protection against temptations and influences

- ◆ Open to attack or assault
- ◆ Weak in the matter of defense

Sounds scary. If you see yourself in or near this condition, you must immediately move toward help and healing. Whatever it takes, do not allow yourself to be the target of these destructive tactics. The devil is not playing games. He has come to destroy your testimony.

Paul says to arm yourself. He urges us to don the belt of truth (Eph. 6:10–18). We arm ourselves by getting a good grip on our situation, by getting some clarity about the battle taking place over our lives. God's intentions toward us are life. Those intentions are opposed. Until we come to terms with war as the context of our days, we will not understand life. We will misinterpret 90 percent of what is happening around us and to us.[2]

The reason Paul instructed us to put on the whole armor of God is because this is warfare. If it wasn't war, he would have suggested we dress casually. Just wear some shorts and a T-shirt. Yet he didn't. He said put on the *whole* armor. This is serious, and you must become serious about your well-being, about your protection, and about your victory. When the smoke clears and the dust settles, you must be the one standing with your foot on the neck of the pernicious one!

Life is not a game show. When this "contest" concludes, the winners and losers will not walk out of the arena arm-in-arm to share an evening of fine dining and entertainment. This is war, and the one with whom you spar doesn't want to fellowship with you; he wants to destroy you! Jesus warns us that this enemy has come to kill, steal, and destroy (John 10:10).

David is a great example for us in warfare. Most of our Christian life we have heard about or studied about young David and his encounter with Goliath. The Bible account takes us into King Saul's palace where Saul is insisting that David wear the king's armor (1 Sam. 17:38–39), but "David took them off."

I don't think David refused the king's armor because it did not fit or even because he had not tested it. David could have had any armor he desired. He had the king's attention. Saul would have gladly ordered his master armor designers to fit David with his own personal armor—even designer armor with David's own initials and family crest raised and embossed in gold. Armor was no problem. *David refused armor because he did not intend to fight Goliath.* He knew he was no match for Goliath in hand-to-hand combat. He had no intention to take him down to the ground or spar with him with swords. David had no intention of fighting the giant. *David intended to kill him!*

The winner here wasn't going to receive a gold trophy with some honoring words engraved on it. The winner of this life-or-death conflict was going to walk away with the loser's head and a total victory for those he represented. David's victory was a victory for himself, his king, his family, his nation, and his future. He was on his way to the throne, and Goliath was in his way!

It is interesting how most people spend years and possibly even a lifetime battling the same enemies of their life. Usually they are the same enemies because we tend to be vulnerable at the same place. We don't have a multitude of places we fail, just the same place multiple times. The reason this same enemy returns to taunt us and tempt us and distract us again and again is because we haven't completely annihilated him and taken off his head. The reason most Christians spar with their enemy rather than annihilate him is because in some hidden, secret recess of their mind, they enjoy what the enemy offers. Somewhere in our clear-mindedness and in our times of wisdom and prayerful meditation before God, we know we have left some doors open to demonic trafficking. We know that offense, unforgiveness, or woundedness are open doors that attract Satan, but we don't completely close them because somewhere in the future we may use them as leverage. We save them down deep in our soul-wound bank because down the road they just might "get me my way." We know that some of those sensual thoughts and sexual temptations are evil and are certainly not of God, but we refuse to totally slam the door to that demonic trafficking because some of these thoughts and imaginations and possibly actions "make me feel good." We lay our head in the lap of Delilah time and again, as did Samson, thinking that we are somehow in control and at anytime we can jump up and free ourselves from the trap.

So we live our lives with doors left open to defeat, frustration, anger, division, and distress because we haven't cut that enemy's head off. We could. Each Christian has been given weapons from God and the armor of God "with which you will be able to extinguish all the flaming arrows of the evil one" (Eph. 6:16) and "be able to stand firm against the schemes of the devil" (v. 11). "For our struggle is not against flesh and blood, but against...spiritual forces of wickedness in the heavenly places" (v. 12). We are made strong in the power of Christ, knowing that "the weapons of our warfare are not of the flesh, but divinely powerful for the destruction of fortresses...destroying speculations [casting down imaginations (kjv)] and every lofty thing raised up against the knowledge of God...taking every thought captive to the obedience of Christ" (2 Cor. 10:4–5).

Be certain that whatever soulish wound we hold dear or whatever temptation we embrace was brought to us by the enemy, scheming to use every opportunity afforded him to kill, steal, and destroy. John reminds us that Jesus came to us and appeared among us "for this purpose, to destroy the works of the devil" (1 John 3:8).

Use every weapon that Christ has given you to make sure that happens. It's not a game. Someone is going to be defeated facedown in the dust, and someone is going to be standing as victor with a head in his hand!

Somewhere in Paul's massive heart and passion for God he found a way to shake off of himself the deep physical and emotional wounds of those who hated him and the disappointments of those who he thought loved him.

Paul had led most of the Corinthian church out of a wicked idolatrous life into a saving knowledge of Christ. Many of these people whom he had established in faith by his powerful preaching and miracle ministry began to hate him. The heresy of the Judaizers had so invaded and permeated the church in Corinth that he couldn't visit them for fear of physical harm. We read how Titus had intervened for Paul and proven the heretics wrong and opened the eyes of these Christians to the truth. Paul was comforted, overjoyed, and returned to them once again: "And not only by his coming but also by the comfort you had given him. He told us about your longing for me, your deep sorrow, your ardent concern for me, so that my joy was greater than ever" (2 Cor. 7:7, NIV).

How do you deal with life's heavy blows? How do you put away the wounds, disappointments, and frustrations? How do you get over these assaults? To be wounded from without is one thing, but to be wounded from within, from those you have trusted, served, to whom you have poured out your life and love—that's something else. But it happens. It happens a lot. It happens too much.

But if you're going to face your crisis with any hope of victory, there is no alternative but to find a place and a way to be healed from these soul wounds. Otherwise the weight of these issues and the disease of these open wounds will bring you to unbearable weariness. And the wearier you become, the more vulnerable you become. At this point in your weary and vulnerable condition, you will be more likely to listen to the whispers of the enemy, and you will begin to embrace them as truth. Whispers like:

+ "It's hopeless."

+ "No one else cares about this relationship."

+ "No one notices how hard I work."

+ "No one appreciates me."

+ "No one else gives the way I do."

+ "No one else works around here."

+ "My prayers are never answered."

+ "God doesn't care."

+ "I could never be forgiven of that."

♦ "No one understands."

When you are weary and vulnerable, it is so easy to embrace these whispers as reality. When you are under this relentless attack, you must put a filter over your mind and ears and put a guard over your mouth. As long as these remain only whispers from the devil, they fall hopelessly to the ground as lifeless dust under your feet. There is *no* power of life or death in *his* mouth. However, if in your weary and heightened vulnerable condition your enemy can convince you to say these things, these words take on an entirely different energy because in *your* mouth is the power of life and death. When the devil whispers complaints, self-pity, murmurings, criticisms, judgments, and temptations, be aware. It's bait! Don't bite. Put a guard over your mouth and only speak words of life and encouragement, or don't speak at all.

"You were tired out by the length of your road, yet you did not say, 'It is hopeless.' You found renewed strength, therefore you did not faint" (Isa. 57:10). No matter the condition of your life today, do not say, "It's hopeless." It's not hopeless. No matter how dark or difficult is your circumstance today, it's not hopeless as long as Christ is invited into your circumstance. When Christ shows up, nothing stays the same. How could it? Invite Christ into your weary condition. Trust Him. God still answers prayer, and He cares very much about you. He will not come and judge your past; He will come and forgive your past and give you a future. When Christ shows up, a miracle shows up. Everything changes. Christ is a miracle in Himself. It may not seem to change immediately, but it cannot remain the same.

The change has begun for you right now. The power and presence of the Lord in your circumstance will bring hope and life. Do not faint. Do not allow your vulnerability to cause you to say words you shouldn't say. Speak life. Pray words of hope. Declare good things over yourself. Your harvest is on the way!

Chapter 9

WHO'S IN YOUR HUDDLE?

I WILL NOT SPEAK much more with you, for the ruler of the world is coming, and he has nothing in Me" (John 14:30). Here Jesus is in conversation with His disciples, a conversation concerning His death and subsequent resurrection. He's assuring them, as He assures us, that He will never abandon them. As He is talking, He becomes aware that the devil, the prince of this world, is coming near, and Jesus says, "I'm not going to talk anymore right now; he will find out nothing from Me" (author's paraphrase).

Here's an interesting insight about this verse: if the devil is coming, then he must not be here. Too many times we ascribe to the devil attributes of deity. Only God is omniscient (all wise), omnipotent (all powerful), and omnipresent (everywhere all the time). These are attributes of God and God alone. Quite evidently the devil wasn't around Jesus and the disciples as they were openly talking because Jesus recognized the devil was coming and stopped talking so He would reveal nothing to "the ruler of this world."

The devil isn't everywhere all the time. We, like Jesus, should be aware when the devil is coming. We should be discerning and be sensitive about the spirits that are around us, when they are around us, and when they are not. Have you ever walked into a room full of people and just felt something wasn't right in the room? Don't take that lightly. You were possibly discerning spiritual things. The Holy Spirit gives you the ability to discern spirits. I've often said, "I'm not so interested in who's in the room; I'm more interested in who is *in* whom in the room!" We must take this example from Jesus and discern when the "ruler of this world" is coming or is near.

Have you ever played sandlot football and found someone sneaking over into your huddle? Why are they there? They are there to steal your plan and frustrate your play; so is your mortal enemy, the devil. Jesus says the devil comes to kill, steal, and destroy. However, Jesus comes to give life abundantly.

I've heard people say, "The devil must read my mind!" No, he does not. He cannot read your mind. Yet he has listened to everything you've said over the years, and he has made note of your weaknesses, your sins, your failures, and the places where you've stumbled. The devil doesn't read your mind, and he doesn't have to. He just listens to what you say and sees how you act. This reminds me of a sign I recently read in front of a church, "Take advantage of every opportunity to keep your mouth shut."

Paul teaches us in the great love chapter of 1 Corinthians 13 that "love keeps no record of wrongs" (v. 5, NIV). This is the nature of God's love. God's love keeps no record of your wrongs. Your enemy is exactly the opposite. He has a CD-ROM from hell that keeps record of your every wrong and remembers your every confession of fear and doubt. The devil doesn't have to read our minds; he just reads our record. We have told him almost everything he needs to know.

The devil thinks he knows exactly how we will react to every pressure in life, every temptation, and every problem. Now is the time to be wise and discerning, no longer falling into his evil trap. Don't speak or act the way you always have. Confuse him; frustrate him. The next time you're pressured or tempted, begin to worship Christ. Break out of the mold. Live your life from a *redeemed* worldview and win over these circumstances. *Your victory will begin with what you say.*

You may be asking, "How can I know when the evil tempter is near?" The answer is *when you are tempted with evil.* Don't allow your enemy into your huddle, and he won't know the plan. You'll begin to win. Your life will turn into a series of victories. When the smoke clears and the dust settles, you'll be standing with your foot planted firmly on the neck of the pernicious one, and he'll be the one thrown over. We've been promised victory as Christians; let's not continue to give the plan away into the enemy's hands.

What has caused you to lose heart? Why are you weary?

Something or someone has disappointed or discouraged you. Someone you believed in has failed, rejected, or has been unfaithful to you. You've been offended or betrayed. You're holding on to something painful along your life's road.

The Dow Jones averages are down, and so are you! That goal you worked toward for retirement has had to be extended. The economy has tanked and taken you with it. You may be involved in a prolonged physical, financial, or emotional battle. You didn't get that raise. You deserved that promotion. Someone humiliated you and held you up for ridicule. You may be fighting an intense temptation, or you may have fallen into sin. You've lost heart and are considering throwing up your hands and quitting.

Life isn't full and fun anymore. You used to laugh so easily. Now laughter is so distant and infrequent. You awake in the night and stare at the ceiling. Rest seems to escape you, and when the day finally breaks, you curse the morning. Thankfulness and worship were at one time a part of your very makeup, but they are now so foreign to you. Something is wrapping around you like a cloak, suffocating you. Dread is setting in. You want to run, but you have discovered you can't run from yourself. You have tried that before and found that wherever you go, there you are.

You have some big choices to make, and you must make them now. You are in spiritual warfare for your heart, your harvest, and your future. You are losing heart, and you need the refreshing that only the Lord can give. You must turn toward your enemy, identify it, and win over this attack on your life and legacy.

The most effective way to deal with weariness is to define what is making you weary. The good doctor can never prescribe until he has diagnosed. Once the medical team makes the diagnosis, they can ably lay out a plan for your healing and ultimate well-being. Spend some time before the Lord and ask Him to reveal to you when your weariness began. What started this? When and how was the door opened to your soul that has allowed your enemy to drain your joy, vigor, and passion for life? The Lord will help you. When you define what has brought this on, then you can begin to put an anointed plan into action to allow Christ to bring you freedom and deliverance.

You will get better. The Lord is faithful. He will answer your prayer and guide you out. Upon the occasion of David's victory over the Philistines recorded in 1 Chronicles 14:11, he exclaims, "'God has broken through upon my enemies by my hand, like the breakthrough of mighty waters.' Therefore they named that place Baal-Perazim." *Baal-Perazim* is translated "the Master of the Breakthrough." Jesus Christ is the Master of your breakthrough!

Chapter 10

THE POWER OF WORDS

NEVER UNDER ESTIMATE the power of your words. In 2008 our church celebrated its twenty-fifth anniversary. During our anniversary week celebration, I invited Dr. Roy and Pauline Harthern to be our special guests in one evening service. Dr. Harthern and Pauline greatly influenced Sandra's and my life as we sat under their ministry for five years. I served in the church for three years and then was brought on to the pastoral staff for two years until we came to the place of our present ministry. These were vital years in my young, preacher life. I did not necessarily enjoy the pressure of discipleship or the demands that were part of the mentoring process while I was there, but I have looked back upon those years as formative and critical to the way we do ministry even today. I'm most grateful for Roy and Pauline Harthern.

That evening of our anniversary celebration Dr. Harthern decided to share his miraculous testimony of physical healing rather than preach. During the darkest days of sickness, his kidneys had completely collapsed and disintegrated, but he had been completely healed by the miraculous restorative touch of God to re-create them right before the doctor's eyes! Dr. Harthern told of his and Pauline's unwavering faith in a faithful God. It is a most dynamic testimony.

I mention this occasion not only because we love them and enjoyed them immensely (Roy even played the piano and he and Pauline sang) but also because of a powerful comment Dr. Harthern made during his presentation. He spoke of the power of words in relationship to health, healing, and well-being. He noted that he was aware of the damage that has been done by the extreme "name it and claim it" doctrines, but he shared forcefully how important is the balanced Bible truth of the power of words.

I remember in the late 1970s as Pastor Harthern would preach on faith and say, "Your faith level will never rise above the words that pass across your lips." That statement is a major plank in the platform of my belief system. The Bible is clear about the power of your words.

> We all stumble in many ways. If anyone is never at fault in what he says, he is a perfect man, able to keep his whole body in check. When we put bits into the mouths of horses to make them obey us, we can turn the whole animal. Or take ships as an example. Although they are so large and are driven by strong winds, they are steered by a very small rudder wherever the pilot wants to go. Likewise the tongue is a small part of the body, but it makes great boasts. Consider what a great forest is set on fire by a small spark. The tongue also is a fire, a world of evil among the parts of the body. It corrupts the whole person, sets the whole course of his life on fire, and is itself set on fire by hell.
>
> —James 3:2–6, niv

> Out of the same mouth come praise and cursing. My brothers, *this should not be*. Can both fresh water and salt water flow from the same spring? My brothers, can a fig tree bear olives, or a grapevine bear figs? Neither can a salt spring produce fresh water.
>
> —James 3:10–12, niv, emphasis added

James uses two examples to demonstrate the power of words:

+ *The bridle in the horse's mouth*—the direction we guide the bridle to turn the horse's mouth is the direction the horse's entire body follows.

+ *The rudder of a ship*—a very small rudder determines the direction and destination of this very large vessel.

Then James says, "...so also the tongue." Verse 6 teaches us the power of our words from a negative point of view. Then he warns us in verse 10 that "these things ought not to be." I have taken the liberty in my Bible to underline the words in verse 6 to bring out the positive message of James's point. It reads like this: "The tongue is set among our members as that which sets the course of our life."

Your words set the course of your life. That's undeniably the point James is declaring. Your words have great power and authority in setting the course of your life. Your words create. One of the first creations of your words is the atmosphere.

I often tell of an incident that happened while my wife, Sandra, and I were in the car traveling from Titusville to Orlando. I had an important call to make on the cell phone and asked her to look on her phone directory and give me the number. However, Sandra was occupied with something she was searching for in the glove box. Because I did not think she was responding quickly enough to my request for a phone number, I reached over and with a flick of my wrist popped the glove box closed while making some remark about how much more important my phone call was than whatever she was doing.

Immediately I created the environment—a very negative one! It turned real cold in the car. All the warmth, along with all the oxygen, immediately emptied out of the cabin. If the car had been an airplane, the oxygen masks would have dropped from the ceiling.

I do not use this occasion to imply this is the only time I have ever said something insensitive but to demonstrate the ability we have to create atmosphere by the power of our words.

You do it often. Consider the comments you make when you sit down at the table for a meal. Someone has set the table, someone has cooked a meal, and someone has put forth an effort however small or large to create this moment. What you say will set the tone for dinner. A word of grumbling or complaint, and the atmosphere becomes tense, the fluids in your body refuse to cooperate, and every bite, no matter how well the food is prepared, is dry and difficult to swallow.

Our words have not only created atmosphere, but they have also given direction to our body as to how it functions. Our physiological being responds with heartburn. On the other hand, the simplest meal of bologna and chips can be a sweet and joyous celebration. A simple thank-you or some expression of gratefulness brings such delight, producing laughter, conversation, and physical well-being. The simple sandwich sets well.

That is not all we create. Our God-inspired creative ability reaches much further. Think of all our words. A word of encouragement to our children as they go out the door to the school bus or a word of appreciation to our spouse, our coworkers, our family of faith creates a life-giving environment. We create environments and atmospheres with our words. There is great power in what we say—not only in creating atmosphere but also in creating faith toward God that relates to every dimension of our lives. Faith is in your mouth. The faith that centers up in your heart is expressed and lived out by the words you say.

> But the righteousness based on faith speaks as follows: "DO NOT SAY IN YOUR HEART, 'WHO WILL ASCEND INTO HEAVEN?' (that is, to bring Christ down), or 'WHO WILL DESCEND INTO THE ABYSS?' (that is, to bring Christ up from the dead)." But what does it say? "THE WORD IS NEAR YOU, IN YOUR MOUTH AND IN YOUR HEART"—that is, the word of faith which we are preaching.
>
> —Romans 10:6–8

In 1990 I began a daily radio program we call *Thee Morning Drive*. The program is live and broadcasts from 6:30 to 9:00 a.m. That's a lot of radio. For the first fourteen years I was the sole host every day. In 2004 my son and partner, Jason, began hosting the Monday and Wednesday editions. That is a refreshing break for me and for our listeners. We are based out of WPIO-FM in Titusville, Florida, and are embraced by many FM stations along the coast, across the state, and into other states. In all of the years and for all the years to come that we're blessed to be on radio, we have committed that our words would be words of blessing and encouragement to our listeners. I can honestly say that has never wavered. Day in and day out, and morning after morning, we share the Word of God, play some music, and celebrate the goodness of the Lord. Someone has categorized *Thee Morning Drive* as "the spiritual breakfast" for thousands of people every morning.

I mention this because these years of positive faith words are seeds planted into the airways and into the hearts and minds of men and women that reap a harvest back into our lives. Not only from the radio but also from the pulpit and in my personal life I am committed and careful to put a guard over my mouth and be mindful of my words. I am not perfect in this arena, but I'm aware of how powerful these spoken words are in relation to the results in my life. I truly believe I live in the harvest of these words. There is no natural reason or explanation for Sandra and me to be as blessed as we are in every area of our lives. I often say, "I'm the most blessed man in the world." I know how insufficient I am to bring about the beautiful grace of God on my life as He has poured it out. I know it's because Sandra and I learned years ago to give bountifully and to speak words of life over ourselves and over others. I know that's true. You can argue with my doctrine, but you can't argue with my testimony. These principles have been planks in the platform and the foundation of our lives, and God proves Himself faithful time after time. God is faithful to His promises.

While I'm sharing these very personal values, allow me to add one more. Along with faithful financial giving and the faith words we speak, I believe we're blessed because we have put our hands on God's assignment for our lives. We were obedient to begin our church in 1983 when we didn't even own a car. We lived in an apartment so small that you could almost touch each side with your arms outstretched. It was very small, but we were excited. We knew when we accepted a small group of people we were touching the will of God for our lives. We didn't see it all laid out in front of us and certainly could not see God's full plan, but we knew by faith we had embraced God's will for us.

Over the years things have not always been easy, but we have seen God's hand of blessing on each step and decision of our lives. Now almost thirty years later, New Life Christian Fellowship—an interdenominational, multicultural fellowship—pastors nearly two thousand families. Those same people who began with us serve on our advisory council, and we have the same treasurer we had from the beginning!

I promise this is not because I'm smart enough to do all these things and to come to this grand place in our lives on my own. It's because the Lord is faithful and because we put our hands to God's assignment for our life's work. The Lord blesses what He's doing. You don't have to beg God to bless what He's doing. The blessing and the success are inherent. You just have to be willing and obedient: "If you will be willing and obedient, you shall eat the good of the land" (Isa. 1:19, nkjv).

All of these blessings are the harvest of seed. Your giving is seed. Your faithfulness to your assignment is seed. Your words are seed. You reap what you sow. Be sure you're living a life you want to reap. Be sure you're sowing words you want to reap. You'll live in the harvest of what you sow. Today you're living in the harvest of the seed you planted a while ago. If you don't like your harvest, begin to plant different seed. If you seed words and actions you want to harvest, you can have a marvelous life.

PART TWO

THE MASTER'S KEYS

Over these next pages I would like to be a voice into your life that helps you identify where to put these seven vital revelation keys that will release you from the weight that has brought you to a place of weariness and has caused you to consider giving up. You have the keys; the Lord has given you the keys to the Kingdom. He invites you to use them to get yourself free.

KEY #1	THE KEY OF AUTHORITY
KEY #2	PURSUE YOUR ASSIGNMENT
KEY #3	RECEIVE MERCY
KEY #4	GET UNDERSTANDING
KEY #5	WAIT
KEY #6	REPENT
KEY #7	CONSIDER JESUS

Chapter 11

THE MASTER'S KEYS REVEALED

Now when Jesus came into the district of Caesarea Philippi, He was asking His disciples, "Who do people say that the Son of Man is?" And they said, "Some say John the Baptist; and others, Elijah; but still others, Jeremiah, or one of the prophets." He said to them, "But who do you say that I am?" Simon Peter answered, "You are the Christ, the Son of the living God." And Jesus said to him, "Blessed are you, Simon Barjona, because flesh and blood did not reveal this to you, but My Father who is in heaven. I also say to you that you are Peter, and upon this rock I will build My church; and the gates of Hades will not overpower it. I will give you the keys of the kingdom of heaven; and whatever you bind on earth shall have been bound in heaven, and whatever you loose on earth shall have been loosed in heaven."

—MATTHEW 16:13–19

No MATTER HOW different your house or apartment may look from every other dwelling in your community, there is one thing all households have in common. In every house there's a drawer, cabinet, or box that holds a wide variety of keys. Some people have a few of these, and some have quite the collection. But no matter where they're stored or how different in age, size, or appearance, they all have this in common: no one knows where these keys are supposed to go. They're worthless because no one knows what they are designed to unlock. Yet we refuse to dispose of them because possibly, one day, somewhere the lock will appear and the key will be useful again.

In Matthew 16 Jesus gives us master keys to His kingdom

treasures. However, these keys can seem worthless to us if we don't know where they fit or how to use them. As long as we trudge around in our carnal ways, we will never know the value of the keys and where they should go because Jesus said "flesh and blood does not reveal this to you."

To find where these valuable keys from Jesus go, we must walk in a dimension of revelation. Flesh and blood does not reveal this to you; God reveals this to you. If He does not reveal this to you directly, He will use an apostolic word from an anointed man or woman of God to reveal these things to you.

The goal is to take these valuable keys and place them into the proper place so you can "bind and loose" or lock and unlock. That's what keys are for. They are designed to lock and unlock; we must know where they go. You have a key to unlock the fullness and happiness in your marriage, to unlock the miracle power of your healing and health, or to move you into that proper place for future wealth and prosperity. You have a master key to your promotion, to great favor and blessing, and to every promise of God in His Word. They are in your possession. You simply need to move in a dimension of Holy Spirit revelation to know when, where, and how to use them.

As I begin to unfold to you the Master's keys in the next several chapters, proceed prayerfully and believe that the Lord will reveal to you where to place these keys. Christ didn't give us keys to frustrate us but to release us into His total design for our lives.

Chapter 12

KEY #1: THE KEY OF AUTHORITY

> Truly I say to you, whoever says to this mountain, "Be taken up and cast into the sea," and does not doubt in his heart but believes that what he says is going to happen, it will be granted him.
>
> —MARK 11:23

T HE POWER OF your words directed toward your mountain will keep you from growing weary.

And on the morrow, when they were come from Bethany, he was hungry: And seeing a fig tree afar off having leaves, he came, if haply he might find any thing thereon: and when he came to it, he found nothing but leaves; for the time of figs was not yet. And Jesus answered and said unto it, No man eat fruit of thee hereafter for ever. And his disciples heard it.

—MARK 11:12–14, KJV

Here, Mark gives us insight into Jesus's encounter with a barren fig tree. We read here that whatever the problem Jesus was experiencing with the tree, He evidently felt it needed to be spoken to. It needed to be addressed. Jesus was in a crisis; He was hungry. He may have been embarrassed by the barrenness of the tree, disappointed, or perhaps He felt deceived or rejected. We may never know the why behind it, but He turned to the tree and spoke to it. It must have been saying something to Him.

Is your crisis saying something to you? Is it screaming at you? You must answer it. It will not just go away. You cannot ignore it. Turn to it and say something. What you say will determine the harvest that comes out of this crisis.

Don't scream at it. Flesh screams, but faith speaks. Speak to it. Give your crisis direction. Tell it what to do. Speak words of faith; speak words of life over your circumstance. Inject your problem with words of faith. Speak to your mountain and expect it to move out of your way, to be *cast into the sea*.

The mountain that is on your shoulders, suffocating your joy in life, needs you to speak to it. It is not intelligent. A mountain only knows to be a weight. It only knows to bear down upon you with relentless pressure. That is what mountains do. They are big, they are heavy, and they are designed to crush you. However, I have good news for you. You are the one with authority over the mountain. Jesus gave you the directive and the authority to speak to it. Why are you so silent? Why do you sit there under the crushing misery of those pressures in your life that have amassed upon your mind and emotions? You aren't that silent about other things. You are passionate about the ball game on Saturday; you speak freely with your family and friends. You are a good person and an intelligent Christian with the power and authority of Christ inside you. Speak to your mountain. Speak to that circumstance that is overwhelming you. Speak to it in the name of Jesus Christ, and command it to move off your shoulders and out of your life forever.

Faith is in your mouth. You have the power of the Word of God in your mouth, but you must release that power with your words. Your words are potent! Speak to that offense, speak to that unforgiveness; speak to that disappointment, that bitterness, that failure, and move it out of your life and out of your way. It is preventing you from moving forward. Cast it into the sea!

When you first speak to it, it may not seem to be responding. Jesus spoke to the fig tree, and it was not until He came back by the next day that His disciples noticed that the tree had obeyed Him. The Lord wasn't worried. He knew it had to obey. He wasn't surprised. He expected it to wither away. It may have taken some time, but it obeyed. So will your mountain obey. Speak to it in faith and believe that you have what you say. Start confessing that you have what you say. Confess that you are not bitter anymore. Confess that you are not offended anymore. Confess that failure is not going to dominate your mind and emotions and decisions anymore. Do not allow your past to dictate your future.

When you speak to your mountain, begin to act like you believe what you say. You will one day realize your mountain is gone. You are free. The weight is gone. You are no longer under the circumstances.

Chapter 13

KEY # 2: PURSUE YOUR ASSIGNMENT

> And He told them a parable, saying, "The land of a rich man was very productive. And he began reasoning to himself, saying, 'What shall I do, since I have no place to store my crops?' Then he said, 'This is what I will do: I will tear down my barns and build larger ones, and there I will store all my grain and my goods. And I will say to my soul, "Soul, you have many goods laid up for many years to come; take your ease, eat, drink and be merry."' But God said to him, 'You fool! This very night your soul is required of you; and now who will own what you have prepared?' So is the man who stores up treasure for himself, and is not rich toward God."
>
> —LUKE 12:16–21

To be successful in the eyes of the world or even in our own estimation is not to be equated with being successful in the eyes of God. There are people elevated by Hollywood and celebrated by the world who are insignificant when it comes to fulfilling any needs of the world. They fly around in private jets, ride in limousines, and pose for photo ops but bring nothing of importance to the world. They are beautiful, rich, well dressed, surrounded by admirers but certainly insignificant. They have no assignment. They are bankrupt in the eyes of God. God doesn't have an issue with them being rich. He takes issue with whom they are rich toward: "This is how it will be with anyone who stores up things for himself *but is not rich toward God*" (Luke 12:21, NIV, emphasis added).

God's definition of a fool is someone who stops at success and doesn't move upward into significance. Jesus called the successful

59

landowner a fool. He didn't call him a fool because he was successful. It is God who gives the ability to succeed. He called him a fool because he was blinded by and took comfort in his own success. He assumed he had reached the pinnacle of his life and was content to sit back and keep filling his barns. He was wallowing in his success, a success that could have been so beneficial to his neighbors, his community, to the gospel, and to the world. This fool's inability to see beyond his barns prevented him from an upward move toward significance. God's plan for the rich landowner and for each of us is to manage each God-given success into a life that would usher us into significance—a mind-set not centered on oneself but one that reaches upward toward God and outward toward others. Success is defined by how my riches serve me. Significance is defined by how my riches serve others.

I think it's interesting that most teaching or preaching I've experienced concerning this parable assumes that this rich man died that night and was thrown into everlasting darkness. That assumption comes from the words God said to him: "This night your soul will be required of you" (v. 20, NKJV). That sounds plenty scary, but it is not necessarily final because Jesus doesn't say it is. I find that many nights and quite often during the day my soul is required of me. God inventories my soul. I think it's noteworthy that the parable doesn't say that God inventoried the rich man's barns. God didn't mind that he had barns full of grains and valuable goods. The man didn't have a barn problem; he had a soul problem!

I often have a soul problem. As a matter of fact, most of my problems center up around my soulishness—what I think, what I want, and what I feel. If it weren't for my soul, I'd be a pretty good guy. But I trip over what I think, what I feel, and what I want. The Lord doesn't require that I look at my barns; He requires that I look at myself. He does inventory, and in doing so He touches every area in me that I have reserved to serve only me. Inevitably, at the conclusion of every inventory session, He asks me the same question He asked the barn stuffer: "Larry, now whom does this belong to? Who owns what you have prepared?" I get it.

Just in case you don't get it, let me help you with the answer because it's important that you get this answer correct. This is a test you need to pass. When the Lord touches secret areas you have reserved for yourself and asks, "Who owns what you have prepared?", answer "You, Lord. It all belongs to You."

Jesus is Lord of all you are, all you have, and all you hope to have and become. The Lord owns it all, and all He has entrusted to you is expected to be used by you to serve His purposes. In serving His purposes in the earth, we embrace an assignment that moves us from successful to significant, and in God's opinion it moves us from foolish barn stuffers to wise and significant kingdom partners and world changers.

THE PROMOTION

We often look at someone we consider important and wish we could be promoted to that high position. Yet it is not the promotion that makes one significant. Consider the person who for years has worked faithfully and has been elevated through the corporate levels and has now been assigned the beautiful twentieth-floor corner office with wrap-around views of the city below.

The day for the upstairs move has come. He arrives early before anyone else, except the security guard at the front glass doors and the receptionist who is just taking her place at her kiosk preparing for a busy day flooded with calls that will pour into the corporate office. It seems they already know about his promotion and are glad for him. The security guard walks over and punches the elevator button for him to the twentieth floor without asking. The corporate receptionist seems to smile a bit brighter as he steps onto the elevator. The elevator ascends to the twentieth floor. The doors open, and he steps off.

All is quiet as he makes his way down the hall toward his corner office renovated just for him. He slowly opens the door and walks deliberately across the spacious room, making footprints in the plush carpet. It's beautiful. There's even a fresh-cut flower arrangement on the center table sharing words of congratulations from the

CEO who chose him for this new position in the firm. He steps around his executive desk and sits down in his executive leather swivel chair, one with the high back complete with lumbar support. Things are quiet. It's early. He's pensive. It's surreal. He rubs his hands across the beautiful mahogany wood finish on his executive desk and opens and closes the drawers a few times, impressed with the silky smoothness of their function. He swivels around in his chair, turns toward the wall behind him, and repeats the process on the matching credenza lining the wall behind him where he examines the newly installed computer specially configured to meet his high-level executive demands.

As he looks up above the computer, he notices the beautifully framed art prints and realizes there are many prints in the office and that they all are professionally designed to flow with the exquisite wall covering and window dressing that frames the windows looking out across the city's skyline. He stands and walks over to the beautifully decorated window, adjusts the bamboo blinds, and looks below to the city just now coming alive twenty floors below.

He has come so far. He remembers the years down there on those streets, in that traffic, fighting that sales war. He stares and remembers. He turns and walks across the office to the wet bar area complete with sink and a mirror. He catches a glimpse of a man in the mirror. He smiles, and the image smiles back at him. He stares into that face for a moment, a reflective moment, then moves back across and sits down once again at his desk. He touches the phone that has an entire communications system that puts many people at his beck and call. He wants to push one of the buttons but hesitates because he has nothing executive to say if someone should answer— and someone will answer. That's success.

The twentieth-floor silence is broken by the sound of the elevator door opening and people chatting and laughing as they arrive for work. Time has passed by so swiftly, and the building is now suddenly bursting into activity. He knows his time for quiet reflection is over.

Within minutes there's a tap on his door, and without hesitation the door opens and his executive director enters. She smiles. He stands and walks around his desk to meet her, and they both sit down in the matching leather chairs circling the glass topped meeting table. They exchange a few pleasantries, and he once again shares his appreciation for this opportunity. Their attention quickly is turned toward the manila folder she has brought in and placed on the table—a folder that makes all the difference in his world. In the folder is his assignment, and in the assignment is his significance. In his significance is the continuing fulfillment of his life.

The same is true in your life. You have an assignment. Your assignment will elevate your life into significance. Your assignment will probably not begin with an office on the twentieth floor. It will begin by you doing something valuable, something that makes a difference in someone's life. You have great talent and true value. The Lord is using these words even now to inventory your soul. He doesn't care that your barns are full or empty. He cares that you care for those around you and use all the tools inside you to elevate someone's life. As you use them, as you move out from where you are and do what you can do now, He fills your life with more life.

Working from the twentieth floor isn't so important. Working from *your* floor is important. Start where you are. Do what only you can do. There's treasure inside you that only you possess, and as you release it, you will find Christ's key to release yourself.

There's someone at the nursing home down the street from you who hasn't had a visit from her family for months. Your visit would brighten her world. Make that call and pray over the phone for that person you've thought of recently. Share a promise from God's Word and pour some faith into that person. They need *your* prayer. There's a feeding and clothing center in your town that needs your hands to help. There's a Sunday school class in your church full of little children who need a godly example as a hero. Many of them do not have a mom and dad at home to guide them, and that child's single parent would so appreciate your help. That widow you know would so enjoy a piece of that pie you made. You know you don't need it. There's a shut-in in your town who would enjoy one of your special meals and even more enjoy your company. Write that poetry. Sing that song. Paint that landscape. Take that class. Join that choir. Run for office. Run that 5K. Sail that boat. Fly that plane. Kick that habit. Dream that dream.

Your dreams will become your visions, and your visions will become tangible if they're from the Lord—and they probably are. The Lord will use every Christian in His service and for His purposes, but He will select His true leaders from among the dreamers. *The language of the Holy Spirit is visions and dreams* (Acts 2:17). My dreams don't come in the night. They come in the morning when I am very awake and very aware of Him as I pray and meditate in times of quietness. I dream of great things. I imagine great things. These dreams become visions, and many times throughout my life these visions have become tangible.

If your dreams, imaginations, and visions are from the Lord, many of them will become tangible. They'll become reality. Some of your dreams and visions will be so grand you may think they are ridiculous. But don't throw them away; preserve them and protect them. Let them develop in you. God just may be using you to bring something to reality that He wants to use for His glory in the earth. Don't share these too readily, because they will probably seem silly and even self-serving to those who don't understand. People will ridicule you for big dreams, and you'll be tempted to stop dreaming. There is an abundance of dream-stompers in the world.

Joseph shared his dream with his brothers. Of all people, you would have thought that his brothers—his family—would have been thrilled about his dream. But you know the result of that. They became jealous, ridiculed him, and ultimately sold him into slavery. Yet his dream was born of God, and God used him to bring about the salvation of an entire people: Israel. He suffered for it, and it took nearly a lifetime to develop. But God is faithful.

David's brothers ridiculed him when he came to bring them lunch in their battle against the Philistines. Yet God had sent him there and used him to defeat Goliath and to once again deliver His people. He also used this event to elevate David toward His anointed and ordained destiny, to rule as king over all Israel. Notice it was victory over David's enemy that elevated him to his next level of life.

Never despise the small beginnings (Zech. 4:10). Deliver that lunch. Be busy about obeying the Lord. You may feel insignificant, but God has chosen you. Give Him an opportunity to use you. You won't start at the twentieth-floor executive suite with the high-back swivel chair. You'll most likely start in the basement mailroom. But if you're chosen of God, no one can keep you there. Remain humble before the Lord. Be patient, and the Lord will elevate you. True promotion doesn't come from man; true promotion comes from the Lord.

Like Joseph's assignment, your assignment from God may take time to develop and a lifetime to fulfill. A vision born of God will and *must* take time. David's development took him from the shepherd's field of his anointing to the battlefield of his Goliath, through the cave of Adullam, through half his promise in Hebron and finally to his total purpose as king over all Israel. The process of that journey prepared him for the throne.

It is the process that builds into you the strong components that will keep your ultimate assignment from crushing you. The place of your ultimate positioning from God is a place with so much pressure it will crush you without proper preparation. The journey, however long and tedious, prepares you for your throne of reigning in life. Do not despise the small beginnings. You are on your way. Don't grow weary.

From the time I began in the ministry, I have had a strong pull toward radio broadcasting. I was blessed through all the years to be able to merge radio into my ministry calling. The first church Sandra and I pastored years ago was west of Clermont, Florida. There was a very small 250-watt AM radio station in Clermont. I began a fifteen-minute Sunday afternoon radio program out of that station. I recorded my fifteen-minute program in our small living room in Orlando on a reel-to-reel tape recorder and delivered it every week to the station. My brother still teases me that the station was so underpowered that people would stand outside and repeat what I said on megaphones. He also jokes that I would begin my weekly program with "Hello, world!" We laugh about those small beginnings, but I was thrilled to be on the radio.

Everywhere I pastored I would find a station to allow me to purchase some radio time. I could bore you with all my radio adventures, but they were all exciting to me. They were a fulfillment of an assignment—a dream. When we pastored in Michigan, I began a morning drive program on a local station. I was the first one at the station each morning. I have often thought that the owners probably were not as interested in my program as they were that I shoveled the snowdrifts off of the sidewalks every day before they got there.

In 1990 I was blessed to begin a radio program called *Thee Morning Drive* in Titusville, where we pastor. During these years, along with pastoring an exciting and explosive church, we have involved ourselves in radio ownership and interests in Florida as partners in Day Star Radio Inc. We are on numerous FM stations in Florida and across the United States and stream around the world from 6:30 to 9:00 a.m. Eastern time each weekday morning at www.findnewlife.com.

Just recently, when I gave the invitation at the end of our third service at New Life on a Sunday morning, a man raised his hand for salvation and came forward with tears in his eyes to give his life to Christ. He informed us that he had been listening to *Thee Morning Drive* for twelve years, and now had a crisis in his life and felt he could come to us—a safe place—for help. There were twelve years of speaking into this man's life before he came to Christ.

I have a letter I keep close from a listener in Pensacola, Florida, who had completed all of his plans and was ready to end his life. One morning while listening to the program, he was convicted of God, pulled his car over to the side of the road, repented, and gave his life to Christ. I was blessed to meet that man. He's a great Christian and contributor to that radio station.

I am not telling you these personal experiences to build me up but to build you up. You may not have ever heard of me until now. I am not a worldwide personality. I face my challenges and problems in life just as you do. Yet there are people in heaven today because I had a dream that turned into a vision that became tangible and real. I dreamed a godly dream. When you and I see Jesus one day, we are not going to hear Him say "Well done, good and rich servant" or "Well done, good and famous servant." We will hear Him say "Well done, good and *faithful* servant."

You do not have to be rich or famous or glamorous to be faithful. You just have to shake off the power of your enemy that has come to destroy your dreams and visions and to trample you into submission and defeat. You have an assignment woven in you with God's fingerprints. It was woven into you as you were forming in your mother's womb. But it is up to you. Pastors can pastor you, counselors can counsel you, prayer warriors can pray for you, and your hair stylist can listen to you, but no one can live your assignment but you.

The cemeteries are full of unrealized, unfulfilled assignments. There is a cure for cancer buried in the cemetery, but people gave up because they couldn't get over the blunt-force trauma life handed them. They grew weary and quit, and the devil stole their dream. He choked their vision, and then he stole their harvest. Don't let this be your story.

Chapter 14

KEY #3: RECEIVE MERCY

Therefore, since we have this ministry, as we have received
mercy, we do not lose heart.

—2 CORINTHIANS 4:1

THE WORD TRANSLATED as "ministry" is the Greek word *diakonia*, which means "serviceable labor." Every business, every calling, so far as its labor benefits others, is a *diakonia*. So whether your assignment in life has you working in the church, in construction, in health care, education, or law enforcement—whatever your life's work is, that's your *diakonia*, because your labor benefits others.

Everyone has a *diakonia*. The point Paul is making here is that along with receiving your assignment for your life, you must at the same time be receiving mercy. You must embrace mercy for yourself and be merciful toward others, or else the pressure of your position will cause you to grow weary and lose heart.

We can best receive mercy as we understand what mercy is. Understand first of all what mercy is not. Mercy is not grace. Grace is wonderful. *Charis*, the Greek work for *grace*, is the undeserved favor of God. You are saved and redeemed by faith through the grace of our Lord Jesus. Through faith in Christ alone we receive salvation, which He has given to us because of His great grace: "God saved you by his grace when you believed. And you can't take credit for this; it is a gift from God" (Eph. 2:8, NLT).

Grace is not mercy. Mercy is translated from the Greek word *eleos*.

Mercy is God's special and immediate regard to the misery
of mankind that results from sin. The lower creation

mankind is the object of God's mercy in as much as the burden of man's curse has redounded upon him. Mercy is God's benevolent pity for the misery brought about by our sin. There may be certain consequences of your past sinfulness that grace may not eliminate. For these consequences, we need God's mercy.[1]

Although you have been redeemed by grace through Jesus Christ, you still must live in and face the consequences of a fallen society. All of that fallenness is not necessarily outside of you. The Holy Spirit lives in you, but the problem is, so do you. It would have been so miraculous if when Christ moved in, all of you would have moved out. But that didn't happen. The process of becoming more like Christ goes on every day. It is the you in you—your carnal nature not yet completely conformed to Christ—that causes you to stumble. It is that human stumbling that causes you to need God's mercy.

We could say grace gets us out of here and mercy gets us *through* here. Grace takes us to the sweet by and by; mercy brings us to some sweet now and now. This understanding of mercy doesn't give you a license to sin. You don't need one; you sin anyway. Your humanness descends upon you sometimes in your thought life, sometimes in your attitudes, sometimes in your actions, sometimes in your marriage, and sometimes in the traffic. That is when you need mercy. Paul says our capacity to receive mercy is one key to keep us from losing heart. When we fail, mercy moves us forward.

I hold myself to a high level of discipline. I expect and demand much of myself. I am driven to excellence. I want things just right in me and around me. I never want to think a bad thought. I never want to struggle with unforgiveness. I never want to trespass God's desires for me. I never want to miss calling someone who is sick or disheartened. I never want to miss reaching a needy person. I never want to preach a bad sermon. I never want to leave my socks on the floor. But all of the above, I do. That's when I need mercy. That's when I must run to the mercy seat. I know God's grace will get me out, but His mercy must get me through. I must not allow my humanness, even my times of fallenness, to keep me from my assignment. I can't quit. Quitting would be the greatest failure. The enemy of your life and harvest will use your failure to drive you out of the race. You are a good person. You are a great example, but you are not perfect. In your imperfection, you must run to the mercy seat.

> Seeing then that we have a great high priest, that is passed into the heavens, Jesus the Son of God, let us hold fast to our profession. For we have not an high priest which cannot be touched with the feeling of our infirmities; but was in all points tempted as we are, yet without sin. Let us therefore come boldly unto the throne of grace, that we may obtain mercy, and find grace to help in time of need.
>
> —HEBREWS 4:14–16, KJV

I Go Home

A few years ago an attorney friend in my church set up a lunch appointment for me with a minister friend of his from Colorado. His friend was "burned out" and was seeking some answers and refreshing from the Lord. As I fellowshiped over lunch with this minister, he began to rehearse to me my busy schedule and then asked me how I could stay refreshed and joyful facing all I had to do. I didn't answer him at first, because what immediately came to my mind didn't seem "spiritual enough." It was not a deeply religious answer, so I just continued to listen until the man asked me again, "How do you stay encouraged and refreshed related to your workload and the pressures of your agenda?"

I thought for a moment and decided to answer him what had first come to my mind. It was a very basic answer. I said, "I go home." I go home. I could see that did not go over very well with him. It was not "deeply religious." I could have said something like, "The Lord Himself comes to me each evening and talks with me as I sit in my study," but that wouldn't have been true.

Part of this minister's problem (which I learned later) was what was going on at home. I am not sure he ever got the point, but I am glad I answered from my heart, because it is the truth. When life gets tough, when I feel wounded or weary out in the world, I love to go home. Home is a place of mercy. *Grace is a place of forgiveness; mercy is a place of acceptance.* I love to go home to my wife, Sandra. When Sandra puts her arms around me and holds me, the whole world becomes a better place. I have not been nor will I ever be a perfect husband, but her mercy heals me. This is why you need both grace and mercy. God's grace forgives you and guarantees your place with Him in heaven, but His mercy allows Him to receive you with all your problems and your fallenness until you get there.

There is no safe place absent mercy. If your attitudes are absent mercy, you are not a safe place. You are a place of unbearable judgment. Perhaps you have unbearable judgment directed toward yourself, to others, or both. That place, absent mercy, will cause you to quit. Life is too hard for us to face without mercy. Think of the places in your life you need mercy from yourself and from God. Be sure you commit yourself more than ever to give and receive mercy. Remember the words of Jesus, "Blessed are the merciful for they shall receive mercy."

Chapter 15

KEY #4: GET UNDERSTANDING

Do you not know? Have you not heard? The Everlasting God, the LORD, the Creator of the ends of the earth does not become weary or tired. His understanding is inscrutable.

—ISAIAH 40:28

S HE DIED IN her sleep. No abuse. Only love. Her parents and grandparents cherished her dearly. But the call came. The seven-month-old baby girl died in her sleep. She just stopped breathing. No funeral is easy, but these are the absolute toughest. The entire atmosphere is filled with "Why?", and so many times these whys turn into anger, anger so often and so easily pointed toward the Lord. My question turned from "Why?" to "What?" What was I going to say to this family and those hundreds of people showing up to offer respect and support?

God does not grow weary because He understands everything. We become weary because we attempt to understand everything and we cannot. You know the list of questions as well as I do.

- Why did she get that promotion when I worked just as hard and am as well qualified?

- Why does he seem to be getting all those blessings in life when I give just as much and have so little to show for it?

- Why does she seem to have her prayers answered and my prayers seem to go unheard?

- Why did their child come to the Lord and mine is still lost in the world?

+ Why does that seven-month-old innocent baby girl die and that old man who has wasted his life continue to live?

This last question was directed to me when I was called upon to officiate at that seven-month-old baby's funeral.

The only answer for these things comes from turning to the Lord and to His Word. I found an answer, at least a few words to say from some scriptures hidden deeply in the twenty-ninth chapter of Deuteronomy. I will take some liberties in the paraphrases.

"All the nations will ask: 'Why has the Lord done this…?'" (v. 24). The entire atmosphere is filled with this question. Why? There's no sin in that question. God doesn't mind. He loves brokenhearted people, and He draws close to them and even to their why. The sin, however, can come in the next verse.

"Then men shall say…*because*" (v. 25, emphasis added). There is a time to say, "I just don't know the answer. This is a tragic situation. My heart is broken along with yours. I don't know why." However, if you have ever noticed, most men will not answer that way. It is too humbling. Our bravado has to have an answer to everything. "So men will say, 'Because…'" It's what they say after the "because" that can turn into heresy. Have you ever noticed how much heresy is pervasive around a funeral? I know we attempt to make the family feel better with our answers, but so many answers can be so wrong on these occasions. "Men will say 'because…'"

Because:

+ God needed another flower in His garden.

+ Someone has sinned, and God is punishing them.

+ Someone lacked the ability to be good parents: "I told them they should have…"

+ They're gone, but they'll come back and visit you each evening. You can talk with them every day.

These are just a few of the tragic misconceptions that come out of death situations. Men do not have to know the answer to blurt out some "because." How good would it be to just keep guard over our mouths in hard times rather than thinking we have to answer every difficult question?

The answer truly comes in verse 29: "The secret things belong to the Lord our God." There are some things you will never know or understand until you see Him face-to-face. No matter how spiritual or knowledgeable someone may tell you he or she is, the secret things belong to the Lord. These are the things we cannot understand, and if we attempt to know these things, they can drive us into depression and a nervous breakdown. These are the questions that awake you in the middle of the night and have you staring at the ceiling in the dark. These are the questions rumbling around inside your head that depress you and bring you guilt. They torment you. They make you weary.

+ If I would have been there...

+ If I would have just checked one more time...

+ If I would have started a few seconds later, I would have not been involved in that accident.

+ If he would have looked before he ran his bicycle into the road...

+ If they had not been traveling so fast...

There are no answers. We grow weary and tormented because we do not understand "the secret things belong to the Lord." You will never know on this side of heaven. However, "The things revealed belong to us and to our sons forever..."

This is a great "however." This "however" is a key that will replace your weariness. Here's where we find peace. Here's a place to exit our weary journey. The things I know—these are the thoughts I center up on. I dwell on these things. The things revealed belong to my sons and me forever.

What do I know?

- ✦ The Lord is good and worthy to be praised. He is the Lord of life!

- ✦ My lost loved one is in heaven eternally. No matter how young or old, they're in a better place.

- ✦ I'll spend eternity with them where we will never say good-bye again.

- ✦ The thief has done this. Jesus has come to "give life and give it abundantly" (John 10:10). Jesus is the life (John 14:6); He is the resurrection and the life (John 11:25).

- ✦ "Life...is even a vapor that appears for a little while" (James 4:14, NKJV). Eternity is what really matters.

- ✦ I can move on. I will heal and recover from this. I do not grieve as those who have no hope. My hope is in the Lord. The Lord is good, and my heart can take hope.

- ✦ "And we know that God causes all things to work together for good to those who love God, to those who are called according to His purpose" (Rom. 8:28).

- ✦ "What then shall we say to these things? If God is for us, who is against us?" (Rom. 8:31).

- ✦ "But in all these things we overwhelmingly conquer through Him who loved us" (Rom. 8:37).

- ✦ "For I am convinced that neither death, nor life, nor angels, nor principalities, nor things present, nor things to come, nor powers, nor height, nor depth, nor any other created thing, will be able to separate

us from the love of God, which is in Christ Jesus
our Lord" (Rom. 8:38–39).

The list of the things revealed is quite endless. The Bible is filled
with them. These are the truths that bring hope, healing, and peace.
They belong to you and to your children forever, and no one can
take them away.

Nations will ask, "Why?" Men will answer, "Because..." But
the Word of the Lord is your strength. "I will lift up my eyes to
the hills—from whence comes my help? My help comes from the
Lord" (Ps. 121:1–2).

Chapter 16

KEY #5: WAIT

> He giveth power to the faint; and to them that have no
> might he increaseth strength. Even the youths shall faint
> and be weary, and the young men shall utterly fall: But
> they that wait upon the LORD shall renew their strength;
> they shall mount up with wings as eagles; they shall run,
> and not be weary; and they shall walk, and not faint.
>
> —ISAIAH 40:29–31, KJV

WHAT A GREAT word of refreshing to the weary! He gives strength to the weary and increases your power. The Lord is your strength, and as you move toward Him and wait on Him, you will find new hope and ability.

Isaiah 40:31 says, "Wait upon the Lord." There are two ways I have observed that you can wait.

1. THE WAITING ROOM

The first way to wait is the way a man waits for his wife while she is shopping. This is *wait* as in *stop*, be idle, relax. Men who have ever done that understand this kind of waiting. If you're weary, you need to get before the Lord and patiently invest some time in quietly waiting for Him. This doesn't imply that He isn't there immediately; there is no place He is not. But it is teaching us to set aside a frame of time and not rush it. To wait here implies your responsibility to take the time to abide in His presence, to be involved in His Word, to worship, to confess, to repent, and to be refreshed in a renewal of your intimacy with Him. If you're weary, giving the Lord a couple minutes of your time will not move you out of your weary condition. Find that place of quiet and aloneness and stay there. When you come out, you'll come out refreshed.

How blessed is the man who does not walk in the counsel of the wicked, nor stand in the path of sinners, nor sit in the seat of scoffers! But his delight is in the law of the Lord, and in His law he meditates day and night. He will be like a tree firmly planted by streams of water, which yields its fruit in its season and its leaf does not wither; and in whatever he does, he prospers.

—Psalm 1:1–3

2. The Serving Room

The second way to wait is best exemplified by those fine people who wait on our table in the restaurant. They serve us and become involved in tending to the details that are important to us. The best servers do this excellently and bring joy to our experience. They deserve a generous tip.

This is the second way we wait upon the Lord. We serve Him. Find a place to serve Him by serving others. A great way to move beyond your personal issues is to involve yourself in someone else's life. There are many people in worse places than you are. Raise up your eyes, look beyond yourself, and see a world full of people who need you and what only you can offer.

Get involved in ministry. Visit the nursing home. Pray with someone in the hospital or in your church. Feed the hungry, clothe the naked, or get involved in prison ministry or missions outreaches in your church.

As you wait on the Lord and as you serve Him through serving others in your church, community, or city, you will be refreshed. Your weary mind, body, and attitude will mount up with strength like an eagle, and you'll find yourself receiving again. You're in the race again. You're winning.

Chapter 17

KEY #6: REPENT

Oh, what joy for those whose disobedience is forgiven, whose sin is put out of sight! Yes, what joy for those whose record the LORD has cleared of guilt, whose lives are lived in complete honesty! When I refused to confess my sin, my body wasted away, and I groaned all day long. Day and night your hand of discipline was heavy on me. My strength evaporated like water in the summer heat.

Finally, I confessed all my sins to you and stopped trying to hide my guilt. I said to myself, "I will confess my rebellion to the LORD." And you forgave me! All my guilt is gone.

—PSALM 32:1–5, NLT

A MINISTER FRIEND OF mine made a statement years ago in a men's prayer breakfast at our church that I will never forget. He said, "You're only as sick as your secret sins." How very true that is. Secret sins open the door to sickness, heaviness, and destruction. Jesus says, "The thief comes only to kill, steal, and destroy." Sin brings death and destruction to our energy, vision, relationships, and testimony. Sin will destroy your legacy: "…lest you give your best strength to others and your years to one who is cruel, lest strangers feast on your wealth and your toil enrich another man's house" (Prov. 5:9–10, NIV).

Hebrews 12:1 says, "Lay aside the weight *and* the sin" (NKJV, emphasis added); therefore, it seems to be clear that all weight is not sin. However, it's possible that many times the weight we carry can center around sin in our lives. How graphically does David describe the weight of sin: "For day and night your hand was heavy upon me; my vitality was drained away as with the fever heat of summer"

(Ps. 32:4). Sin is heavy. Sin is draining. Sin's heaviness will drain your joy, your righteous relationships, your hopes, your energy, your mind, your testimony, and your legacy. Someone has said that sin will take you farther than you want to go, keep you longer than you want to stay, and cost you more than you want to pay.

The answer to growing weary because of sin is quite evident—*Repent*. Repent means to:

+ Think differently about a certain issue

+ Turn completely from the issue

+ Put the issue to your back and never turn around again

Sin seldom begins ugly. It may even begin with delightful and enjoyable thoughts. Sin entices and weaves its web until we are caught in it. Then it stings its demon venom, and we die a thousand deaths. The righteous man dies only once. The sinner dies a thousand deaths. Sin opens the door to demonic trafficking in the Christian's life. It begins in our thought life, seemingly harmless. As we entertain it, it pushes open the door of demonic attack and entertains it further and further. When it is finished, we have demon foot tracks across our backs. "...and sin, when it is finished, bringeth forth death" (James 1:15, KJV).

ATTRACTING THE ATTACK?

Years ago I prayed regularly with a group of pastors in our community. One of the pastors was a lady who told us of an incident in her life when she was young, newly married, and pregnant with her first child. She was busy on her uncle's farm where she and her family were staying, helping with the farm chores. This particular day she was assigned to slop the hogs, a job she had never done but one she felt confident she could accomplish.

While involved in her "sloppy" assignment, she realized that a large sow was becoming very aggressive toward her. The aggressiveness became intense to the point that she felt the need to get away. In her panic, she bolted out the hog pen and began to run for her life!

In her eagerness to get away, she had not shut the gate and found that this massive hog was in close pursuit of her. Her instincts turned her toward the farmhouse a few hundred yards up the road, where her uncle stood on the front porch aware of her dire predicament. She moved into a full run only to realize that the faster she ran, the faster the hog ran. All she could hear was the sound of her young heart pounding, her own footsteps slapping the ground, and the grunting of a massive hog in close pursuit. She could see her uncle on the farmhouse porch in the distance and realized he was trying to communicate something vital to her. She couldn't make out what he was screaming because of all the noises in her head and those close behind. As she approached her uncle, barely ahead of the hog behind her, she finally got close enough to clearly hear his instructions. He was screaming, "Drop the slop!"

In her frantic effort to get out of the pigpen, she not only didn't close the gate, but she also forgot to put the slop pail down. When she let it fall away, the crisis was immediately over and she was safe. She had to let go of what has attracting the pig.

What a lesson for us all. There are things in our lives that attract the attack. The enemy of your life is attracted to the sinful desire you are clutching. He senses it and takes the occasion as an invitation to invade your life. We really do not want what he brings. It would be good for us to kneel our passions, desires, plans, and wishes before our Lord and leave the slop that is attracting our enemy. It is time to slam the door to demonic trafficking. Drop the slop!

Chapter 18

KEY #7: CONSIDER JESUS

For *consider him* that endured such contradiction of sinners against himself, lest ye be wearied and faint in your
minds.

—Hebrews 12:3, kjv, emphasis added

J ESUS IS ALWAYS our greatest example in all things. In Matthew
11 the Master gives us one of His greatest promises: "Come
unto me, all ye that labor and are heavy laden, and I will give
you rest. Take my yoke upon you, and learn of me; for I am meek
and lowly in heart: and ye shall find rest for your souls. For my yoke
is easy, and my burden is light" (vv. 28–30, kjv).

Always remember that the Lord is your ever-present help. He
loves you. He really does. The Lord is not mad at you. He loves
you and draws you to Himself. God isn't against you for your sin;
He is for you against your sin. Jesus is your closest friend. He will
never leave you or forsake you. Recently I was reminded of a song
we sang years ago, "Turn Your Eyes Upon Jesus." The lyrics of this
song address the weary soul and give it direction and encouragement to shake off the weariness.

> O soul, are you weary and troubled?
> No light in the darkness you see?
> There's light for a look at the Savior,
> And life more abundant and free!

> Turn your eyes upon Jesus,
> Look full in His wonderful face,
> And the things of earth will grow strangely dim,
> In the light of His glory and grace.

Through death into life everlasting
He passed, and we follow Him there;
O'er us sin no more hath dominion—
For more than conquerors we are!

His Word shall not fail you—He promised;
Believe Him, and all will be well:
Then go to a world that is dying,
His perfect salvation to tell![1]

It is so easy to become distracted in such a world full of clamor and demands. It is so easy to run out the door each day without honoring our appointment with God. To do so is to lose our focus. Don't allow the pressures of this world to move you away from the good things you know. Keep your eyes on Jesus. Look at everything in the world through Him. Make every decision by including Him. "You will keep him in perfect peace, whose mind is stayed on You, because he trusts in You" (Isa. 26:3, NKJV).

THE WEIGHT ALWAYS WINS

Recently I was surfing through television channels when I came upon a most interesting competition. You have probably seen those tractor-pull competitions that involve very powerful tractors that pull heavy loads racing toward a finish line. These tractors have massively powerful engines—more than one thousand horsepower. The idea of the competition is to attach this beautifully designed tractor to a weight that slides closer to it along a rail as it hurries toward the finish line. The closer the weight moves along the rail toward the tractor, the heavier the load becomes, until the tractor can no longer move, sitting and spinning its wheels and ultimately blowing its massive engine.

This competition reminds me of us. We were created by a glorious and perfect God, in His likeness, designed as "massive machines" to move freely and powerfully toward the finish line. However, we take on the weight of wounds. We carry a load, an accumulation of pain and offenses we have picked up along the road of life. The heavier the load is, the closer we move toward overload and power failure. We sit spinning our wheels or even blowing our engine. No matter the design and no matter the horsepower, you will not get to your desired goal unless you find a way to lighten the burden. You weren't built for the weight; you were built for the race. You can handle some weight from time to time but you weren't designed for it. It will wear you out. It will boil you over. The weight always wins.

You cannot reason or negotiate with the weight. Your problems didn't show up in your life to be reasonable. They were sent by the enemy to crush you and to keep you from the finish line of your harvest and your destiny. The only option you have is to rid yourself of this destructive opponent that has infiltrated your mind and emotions. Remember the key: turn to the mountain and speak to it. It will obey you. It must obey you. Cast it into the sea!

CONCLUSION

As I end this book, I have left you with numerous passages from the Book of Psalms. I have prayerfully and carefully chosen them because I believe they will bring you encouragement and lead you to wholeness. So do not finish this book and put it away. Let its ending become your beginning to breaking free from a rut of weariness and ascending the mountain to new heights in your walk with the Lord. Let this be a manual for you; one that you will refer to often to remind you of the keys that will continuously unlock your victories. Remember, they are *your* keys. Jesus gave them to you to bind and loose and to lock and unlock.

I also want to offer my ministry staff and myself to you to assist you in prayer and encouragement. Our phone number is in this book, as well as our website. We would welcome your call. I will be on the radio each weekday morning from 6:30–9:00 a.m. Eastern time. We stream the program live on the Web at www.findnewlife. com. I will be joined by other radio hosts and by our prayer partners. We can believe God together. We will believe God with you for your overwhelming victory. Give us a call.

Thank you for reading my book. I pray it has helped you in your life and will continue to help you in all your life issues. *Don't grow weary.* You have some great seed to harvest. You are a good person. The Lord cherishes you and rejoices over you. Run the race with endurance. I'll be looking for you at the finish line.

> My soul, wait in silence for God only, for my hope is from Him. He only is my rock and my salvation, my stronghold; I shall not be shaken. On God my salvation and my glory rest; the rock of my strength, my refuge is in God. Trust in Him at all times, O people; pour out your heart before Him; God is a refuge for us. Selah.
>
> —PSALM 62:5–8

O God, hasten to deliver me; O LORD, hasten to my help!
Let those be ashamed and humiliated who seek my life;
let those be turned back and dishonored who delight in
my hurt. Let those be turned back because of their shame
who say, "Aha, aha!"

—PSALM 70:1–3

Teach me Your way, O LORD; I will walk in Your truth;
unite my heart to fear Your name. I will give thanks to
You, O Lord my God, with all my heart, and will glorify
Your name forever. For Your lovingkindness toward me
is great, and You have delivered my soul from the depths
of Sheol.

—PSALM 86:11–13

Bless the LORD, O my soul, and all that is within me, bless
His holy name. Bless the LORD, O my soul, and forget
none of His benefits; who pardons all your iniquities, who
heals all your diseases; who redeems your life from the
pit, who crowns you with lovingkindness and compassion;
who satisfies your years with good things, so that your
youth is renewed like the eagle.

—PSALM 103:1–5

But You, O GOD, the Lord, deal kindly with me for Your
name's sake; because Your lovingkindness is good, deliver
me; for I am afflicted and needy, and my heart is wounded
within me.

—PSALM 109:21–22

The LORD is righteous in all His ways and kind in all His
deeds. The LORD is near to all who call upon Him, to all
who call upon Him in truth. He will fulfill the desire of
those who fear Him; He will also hear their cry and will
save them.

—PSALM 145:17–19

How blessed is the man who does not walk in the counsel of the wicked, nor stand in the path of sinners, nor sit in the seat of scoffers! But his delight is in the law of the LORD, and in His law he meditates day and night. He will be like a tree firmly planted by streams of water, which yields its fruit in its season and its leaf does not wither; and in whatever he does, he prospers.

—PSALM 1:1–3

O LORD, how my adversaries have increased! Many are rising up against me. Many are saying of my soul, "There is no deliverance for him in God." But You, O LORD, are a shield about me, my glory, and the One who lifts my head. I was crying to the LORD with my voice, and He answered me from His holy mountain. I lay down and slept; I awoke, for the LORD sustains me.

—PSALM 3:1–5

Many are saying, "Who will show us any good?" Lift up the light of Your countenance upon us, O LORD! You have put gladness in my heart, more than when their grain and new wine abound. In peace I will both lie down and sleep, for You alone, O LORD, make me to dwell in safety.

—PSALM 4:6–8

I love You, O LORD, my strength. The LORD is my rock and my fortress and my deliverer, my God, my rock, in whom I take refuge; My shield and the horn of my salvation, my stronghold. I call upon the LORD, who is worthy to be praised, and I am saved from my enemies.

—PSALM 18:1–3

He delivered me from my strong enemy, and from those who hated me, for they were too mighty for me. They confronted me in the day of my calamity, but the LORD was my stay. He brought me forth also into a broad place; He rescued me, because He delighted in me.

—Psalm 18:17–19

The Lord is my light and my salvation: whom shall I fear? The Lord is the defense of my life: whom shall I dread? When evildoers came upon me to devour my flesh, my adversaries and my enemies, they stumbled and fell. Though a host encamp against me, my heart will not fear; though war arise against me, in spite of this I shall be confident.

—Psalm 27:1–3

I will extol You, O Lord, for You have lifted me up, and have not let my enemies rejoice over me. O Lord my God, I cried to You for help, and You healed me. O Lord, You have brought up my soul from Sheol; You have kept me alive, that I would not go down to the pit.

—Psalm 30:1–3

I sought the Lord, and He answered me, and delivered me from all my fears. They looked to Him and were radiant, and their faces will never be ashamed. This poor man cried, and the Lord heard him and saved him out of all his troubles. The angel of the Lord encamps around those who fear Him, and rescues them.

—Psalm 34:4–7

I waited patiently for the Lord; and He inclined to me and heard my cry. He brought me up out of the pit of destruction, out of the miry clay, and He set my feet upon a rock making my footsteps firm. He put a new song in my mouth, a song of praise to our God; Many will see and fear and will trust in the Lord.

—Psalm 40:1–3

Why are you in despair, O my soul? And why have you become disturbed within me? Hope in God, for I shall again praise Him for the help of His presence.

—Psalm 42:5

Please receive this psalm as my blessing over you:

May the Lord answer you in the day of trouble! May the name of the God of Jacob set you securely on high! May He send you help from the sanctuary and support you from Zion! May He remember all your meal offerings and find your burnt offering acceptable! Selah. May He grant you your heart's desire and fulfill all your counsel! We will sing for joy over your victory, and in the name of our God we will set up our banners. May the Lord fulfill all your petitions.

—Psalm 20:1–5

NOTES

CHAPTER 1
A WAY OUT

1.   Dave Berman, "Losing Weight to Live," *Florida Today*, September 28, 2010, section D, reprinted with permission.

CHAPTER 4
SEED TIME AND HARVEST

1.   John Eldredge, *Waking the Dead* (Nashville, TN: Thomas Nelson, 2003), 18, 34.

CHAPTER 7
LIVE A LIFE WORTH LEAVING

1.   H.I. Hester, *The Heart of the New Testament* (Nashville, TN: B&H Academic, 1980), 335.
2.   Ibid., 337.

CHAPTER 8
THE LIE WHISPERER

1.   *The American College Dictionary* (New York: Random House, 1974), s.v. "vulnerable."
2.   Eldredge, *Waking the Dead*, 16–17.

CHAPTER 14
KEY #3: RECEIVE MERCY

1.   Spiros Zodhiates, ed., *Hebrew-Greek Key Word Study Bible* (Chattanooga, TN: AMG Publishers, 2008).

CHAPTER 18
KEY #7: CONSIDER JESUS

1.   "Turn Your Eyes Upon Jesus" by Helen H. Lemmel. Public domain.

ABOUT THE AUTHOR

D
R. LARRY LINKOUS is a third generation preacher whose more than forty years of public ministry experiences has sharpened his awareness and sensitivity to the challenges and needs of people in this demanding world. Larry spent his younger years out of Bible school in evangelism and youth ministry, but early on realized his true calling as pastor, a shepherd of God's sheep.

Larry has been married for forty-four years to his wife Sandra and they pastor a growing and exciting inter-denominational multicultural church on the Space Coast of Florida, a church they founded in 1983. In 1990 Larry began a daily two-and-a-half hour radio program *Thee Morning Drive* that continues to broadcast daily Monday thru Friday from 6:30 to 9:00 eastern time airing on many stations across the nation and streaming around the world at www.FindNewLife.com.

Dr. Linkous is also president of Daystar Radio, Inc. with radio interests in Florida and across the nation. He travels and teaches for Beacon University using his first book, *Christ is Better, Don't Go Back*, as the textbook for a class on New Testament grace.

Through his books, radio ministry and his pulpit ministry, Larry shares a unique insight into the life and love of Jesus Christ, His grace and unrelenting love for mankind.

CONTACT THE AUTHOR

YOU ARE ENCOURAGED TO CONTACT
LARRY LINKOUS AND HIS STAFF
BY PHONE AT 321-269-7578.

OR THEIR WEBSITE AT WWW.FINDNEWLIFE.COM.

THE ADDRESS OF THE CHURCH IS:

NEW LIFE CHRISTIAN FELLOWSHIP

6755 S. WASHINGTON AVE.

TITUSVILLE, FL 32780